"David Sammel is an International Tennis Coach and a widely respected Consultant across the spectrum of professional sport. He is the creator of the coaching philosophy that is known as Locker Room Power."

LOCKER ROOM POWER

Building an Athlete's Mind

Author

David Sammel

Copyright © David Sammel 2019

The author has asserted his rights under the Copyright, Designs and Patents Act 1988 to be identified as the author of this work.

This book is sold subject to the condition that it shall not, by way of trade or otherwise, be lent, resold, hired out, or otherwise circulated without the publisher's prior consent in any form of binding or cover other than that in which it is published and without a similar condition, including this condition, being imposed on the subsequent purchaser.

All right reserved.

First published in paperback in Great Britain in 2014 by Westbrook Publishing

Second edition published in Great Britain in 2019.

CONTENTS

Foreword

A Note from David Sammel

Acknowledgments

Introduction

- Chapter 1 -
Locker Room Power - 1

- Chapter 2 -
The Impact of Locker Room Power - 4

- Chapter 3 -
My Coaching Philosophy - 8

- Chapter 4 -
Competitive Mentality - 12

- Chapter 5 -
Play to Gain - 15

- Chapter 6 -
Weapons - 20

- Chapter 7 -
Psychological Statements - 24

Chapter 8 -
Intimidation and Gamesmanship - 28

- Chapter 9 -
Personality used as a Weapon - 32

- Chapter 10 -
Upside down - Is your weakness a strength? - 35

- Chapter 11 -
Radiators - Positive Energy Sources - 38

- Chapter 12 -
Drains - The Energy Sappers - 40

- Chapter 13 -
Self-Consciousness and Body Image - 42

- Chapter 14 -
Fear - 45

- Chapter 15 -
Myth of the Introvert - 48

- **Chapter 16 -**
Anger - 50

- **Chapter 17 -**
Libido - 53

- **Chapter 18 -**
Creating Locker Room Power - 55

- **Chapter 19 -**
Consolidating Locker Room Power - 59

- **Chapter 20 -**
Locker Room Power - Case Study - 61

- **Chapter 21 -**
Complacency & Arrogance - 65

- **Chapter 22 -**
Goals from the Heart - 68

- **Chapter 23 -**
Injury - 73

- **Chapter 24 -**
Courage - 74

- **Chapter 25 -**
Consistent Habits for effective Mind Management - 82

- **Chapter 26 -**
In & Out Of The Zone - 85

- **Chapter 27 -**
Ego and Humility - 87

- **Chapter 28 -**
Separate Self-Belief from Confidence - 89

- **Chapter 29 -**
Desire - 95

- **Chapter 30 -**
Perseverance - 98

- **Chapter 31 -**
Success - 100

- **Chapter 32 -**
Theoretical Underpinning by Louise Scott - 103

- **Chapter 33 -**
Sammelism's - 106

Background & Glossary - 112

LOCKER ROOM POWER

Locker Room Power

FOREWORD

I was fortunate to meet David at the start of the new millennium in rather a surprising environment given his professional background and career history. Dave had been invited in to speak at one of our famous first team away days that Mike Ford and Sam Allardyce organised at Bolton Wanderers throughout the season. This was a very unique gathering. The aim of the day was for sport science staff, first team coaches and the manager to take quality time out to consider immediate problems and explore how we could continue to develop our performance for the future.

There was a tradition of inviting highly successful people from across a range of performance domains to speak to us about how they managed and developed excellence. Dave was the first person from tennis we had encountered. The football fraternity, especially at professional levels, can sometimes give the impression that there is nothing left for them to learn. Within 10 minutes of Dave's opening salvos, most of the twenty-five or so staff in the room had a different view.

A number of very important topics were brought to our attention that day. However, the two that had the biggest impact, in that staff frequently mentioned them in the seasons ahead, were Locker Room Power and Team Weapons. Immediately this terminology appealed to the football coaches and applied psychologists in the room. After Dave had proceeded to explain the importance of these two factors and provided lively and colourful examples of where he had seen these in real world practice, the football staff became excited about how this could be applied to their world.

Much of what Dave said that day, and has continued to say, resonates with those working with high-level performers in particular, and especially in the area of psychology. Although not recognised as a qualified sport psychologist, I have often found his understanding of performance psychology to be well in advance of much contained in research journals and theory. And this is how it should be! This is because Dave has survived and thrived, not on the number of publications he has produced, but because his ideas have helped to develop excellence in practice.

Beyond skillful use of particular techniques and strategies, the most impressive part of Dave's approach is the underlying philosophy. There are many ways this can be described. Maybe one of the best would be to say that it is based on a belief that performing to the best that you can be will come at a cost. And that cost will involve small details and everything else.

Dave's philosophy can be summed up as being somewhat in keeping with the man himself; total commitment, full intensity, all the time, particularly when there is a need to courageously adopt a different way to achieve success. In other words as this book makes clear it is about having a firmness around foundations and ideals, which paradoxically allows the athlete, coach or individual to operate in the flexible and creative way where necessary.

Some of the views contained in this book are quite conventional and generally accepted. Others are much less so. I believe that a good book should always provoke and make us feel uncomfortable. This is usually a sign that we have to wrestle with new ideas and novel concepts. This is actually a description of learning.

Both authors of this book have drawn on their experiences in the sport of tennis and their academic and professional backgrounds to offer something new to the sport. Maybe this is best seen through their account of Locker Room Power. This idea is infused with psychology and yet is very recognisable to anyone who has played tennis and other sports at a good level of performance. We have all lost games in changing rooms although few of us would have wanted to talk about this. But of course, as Dave and Louise remind us here, anyone can learn to win games before they step onto the court or field of play. It is this type of paradoxical yet very frequently experienced scenario that should provide a stimulus to deeper engagement and thinking.

Knowing both authors well it is this final point that they hope their book will achieve. They never set out to have the last word and hope that others will be encouraged to contribute their own understanding of the path to excellence.

Dr. Mark Nesti

Dr Mark Nesti is a reader of Sport Psychology at Liverpool John Moores University. He has produced countless research papers, and books highlighting his work in the applied world of sport.

A NOTE FROM DAVID SAMMEL

This book is essentially a collection of honed and tested methods of applied psychology that I have collected over my sports career. Although I'm not a qualified sports psychologist, my involvement in professional sport as a player and latterly as an elite coach has given me a thorough knowledge of delivering psychological support for athletes across many disciplines. This book is not the kind that you read cover to cover and throw in the back of your draw; it will become your reference to return to again and again as you refine and strengthen your mental toughness and build your own Locker Room Power.

However this book is not only for coaches and athletes - it is for parents and anyone who wishes to improve their performances in any walk of life. What you will gain from this book are insights and practical ideas as to how to achieve excellence, how to create an edge and importantly learn the antidotes to being self-conscious or intimidated by others.

This is not a 'feel good' book, but rather a realistic method of how to approach and apply the work needed to improve and succeed. I believe this is a powerful book and an important contribution to understanding the secrets of mental toughness.

The essence of this book is that I take the complex process of building an athlete's mind by teaching simple and practical tools that help the athlete become mentally tough. In the tennis world, top players are now employing ex-great players to assist them in gaining an edge - using their experience to essentially increase their own 'Locker Room Power'.

Tim Henman says: *"We all know this aura exists. What I like about this book is that you give it an identity."*

I truly hope that you can find your 'Locker Room Power'.

David Sammel

ACKNOWLEDGMENTS

It was a humbling experience when I sat down and thought about who I wanted to thank for being who I am, the type of coach I am, and those who have helped with the book. The number of people who have inspired and helped me is truly amazing and certainly too many to name, so at the outset apologies to anyone I miss out.

Stability and simplicity is very important for focus. I am blessed with a wonderful wife, Joy. She is a fabulous support who has an independence that allowed me the freedom to travel and pursue a career in high performance. Her refreshing approach to life, insight into people and ability to do the right thing is an inspiration to me and frankly keeps me in check. Our daughter Roxanne played high level tennis and is now a physical trainer, so again I'm grateful for her support which allows me to have a wonderful family life in an extremely challenging job which takes me away for over 200 days a year.

My parents were unique for having four natural children and going on to adopt a further six. Their message to us children was "Challenge existing rules and know you can go after anything in life if you put your mind to it". We also learnt quickly that life is messy. When there are ten children there is conflict, resolution, countless issues arising and vastly different viewpoints to navigate. There was a strong hand when chaos became unruly - that being the iron will of my mother. I first became aware of aura or charisma whilst watching my father both socially and in business. He oozed confidence and knew how to use wit and size to intimidate or charm depending in the circumstances. Importantly, he backed it up with substance. He feared little, having survived World War II. He was blessed with an incredibly high IQ coupled with a photographic memory. My mother was athletic and excelled in netball, an accessible sport for a girl from a poor family. She reached the pinnacle when selected for South Africa. She came to tennis late at the age of 26, yet made the top 10 in South Africa by her late 30s.
A remarkable achievement.

She had champion qualities but, self-taught, she came to both tennis (her true love) and badminton too late in life to fulfill her potential, which confirmed to me that being able to achieve anything, no matter what,

Acknowledgements

is a myth. Genetics, opportunity and age hold inherent restrictions, but challenging those restrictions is fun.

I realised from my parents that winning was as much about state of mind as it was ability. Thus, the seeds of "the importance of the mind" were sown into my DNA. I also recognised that opportunity at the right time plays its role and that unguided ability, fight, and bloody mindlessness can only get a person so far.

Everyone needs a coach and periods of smart mentoring.

The journey of writing a book was far longer and far harder than I anticipated. Original help in editing came from Anne Meredith. My sister Joyce Hayward, herself a clinical psychologist, an ex-pupil Venki Sundaram and colleague Jim Edgar all helped cut out fluff and smooth the journey. Special thanks have to go to Nick Baglin who questioned the structure and led me to rethink the entire book. Luckily, in needing help for her Master's thesis, Louise Scott contacted me through Mark Nesti. Her interest and enthusiasm for exploring the psychology of players and parents prompted me to ask if she was interested in doing some research for the book to underpin my practical experience. This became a collaboration that crystallized the book into something I'm truly proud to have finished. Mark Nesti, who mentored Louise and with whom I've worked on and off for ten years, challenges my thinking and works with some of the players that I coach.

I have to thank the players and coaches at TeamBath, who are helping create a truly special programme. I also have to thank the generations of players I have coached, from Amy van Buuren, the first junior I took into the pros, to those who play and played Davis Cup and Federation Cup – Liam Broady, Marcus Daniell, Martin Lee, Andy Richardson, Miles Maclagan, Barry Cowan, Arvind Parmar, Jamie Delgado, Wes Moodie, Chris Haggard, Anna Smith and Sam Murray, through to many who now coach or work in tennis themselves – to name a few Gary Henderson, Kate Warne-Holland, Colin Beecher, Tom Spinks, Colin Bennett and Nicola Payne.

I worked with Jez Green for 11 years and together we pioneered tennis movement pattern training in the late 1990s. Jez left my academy to become Andy Murray's lead trainer in 2007 but his single-minded drive to improve players fitness in conjunction with their minds made us a formidable team. Doing the hard yards is an integral part of developing mental toughness.

I learned and honed my skills in the relentless drive to help players improve. It is a shame that the players could not benefit from all the experience and knowledge gained over subsequent years, but it is a fact of life - we don't know what we don't know. What I am proud of is that I believed in them and never set a ceiling, encouraging them to believe that they could and would play against the best in the world. Many of them did. My coaching evolved with their careers and my philosophy grew. I began to create a culture of excellence, which is now the cornerstone of our programme.

Understanding Locker Room Power is a powerful driver behind the development of a competitive mind. Players and coaches have benefited from this knowledge. Your faith in buying this book, will be repaid in helping you reach a new understanding of mental toughness.

Special Acknowledgment

Louise Scott (Msc and Bsc in Sport Psychology) has been a huge help with research, ideas on structure and clarifications. She conducted the interview with Samantha Murray and was instrumental in assisting me in editing the final version. I look forward to future work with Louise. She is currently Head of Sport Science at Sporting Club Albion.

INTRODUCTION

I've known Dave for about 20 years now and although we have never worked together, I've spent enough time chewing the tennis fat with him to know that his passion and commitment to the game is second to none. He understands the demands of world class tennis and the life a player must lead if they are to become a successful touring pro, so he knows how to instill the kind of values that serve players well on and off the court.

He has helped many wannabe players achieve their dreams and has a particular knack for spotting talent in later bloomers and maximizing that potential. He's even had a hand in the development of ex-player Jez Green into a world-class physical trainer who has worked with Andy for 5 years.

Locker Room Power (LRP) is an example of how Dave continues to observe and absorb lessons from other sports and works them into his own philosophy. We share the same view that humour and fun is important in training as long as you blend it with the right amount of discipline and intensity. LRP is an extremely powerful concept - for players and coaches - and is a major factor in the achievement of consistent success at the top of any sport.

This is a top book by a top coach and an amazing student of the game. Wishing Dave lots of success with his players and with LRP!

Judy Murray

Locker Room Power

- CHAPTER 1 -
LOCKER ROOM POWER

"Never again will I inspire such fear in the locker room."
Andre Agassi

Locker Room Power is a positive aura that surrounds an athlete and can be thought of as the X-factor in competition. LRP is the culmination of practice, intent and commitment. It creates a fear factor that saps an opponent's desire and self-belief. With effective LRP many matches are won before a player steps on court. It can cause opponents to lose confidence during a tough match or allow doubt to creep into their minds in a crisis. It is the ingredient that makes opponents nervous and prone to mistakes.

Simply put, LRP is the myth on top of the reality.

Compared to the other factors - desire, weapons and self-belief - LRP is far less tangible. For instance, you will often hear people attribute success through comments such as 'It wasn't about forehands and backhands; you could just tell he was going to win, he had that look about him' or 'That contest was won before the fight began.'

Andre Agassi understood his aura. In his recent autobiography OPEN he encapsulates the essence of Locker Room Power:

"At last the tournament begins. I win my first four matches without dropping a set. It's evident to reporters and commentators that I'm a different player. Stronger and more focused. On a mission. No one sees this more clearly than my fellow players. I've always noticed the way players silently anoint the alpha dog in their midst, the way they single out the one player who's feeling it, who's likeliest to win. At this tournament for the first time, I'm that player. I feel them all watching me in the locker room. I feel them noting my every move, the little things I do, even studying how I organize my bag. They're quicker to step aside when I walk by, eager to give up the training table. A new degree of respect is directed toward me, and while I try not to take it seriously, I can't help but enjoy it. Better me getting this treatment than someone else."

(OPEN pg. 206)

Other athletes discuss an athlete with LRP positively, which creates an aura of invincibility around the athlete. In sport the talk surrounding a player determines how well his game is perceived.

The following example from an incident early in Tim Henman's career illustrates this. I explained to Henman the essence of Locker Room Power and asked him if he had encountered it during his playing days.

He said, "We all know this aura exists and what I like about this book is it gives it an identity. I was made acutely aware of LRP before a semi-final match against Boris Becker in the Grand Slam Cup, a unique tournament given that each player was given his own locker room. I had beaten Michael Stich and MaliVai Washington and felt confident. The stakes for me were high as it was early in my career and we were playing for $250,000 minimum difference in earnings, plus the chance to beat Becker in Germany. "We walked out of the locker rooms. Boris stood a few metres from me down the corridor. He just shifted from foot to foot, game face on and waited and waited. I became unsure what to do. Wait for him? Go first? Wait him out? In these final moments before the match I became unsettled. I realised afterwards that he totally dictated the time – he sent the message that the match would be played according to his terms."

Locker Room Power doesn't just incorporate the setting of the locker room; it encompasses the whole competition environment.

The locker room not only refers to the changing room but any place where athletes interact and observe. It is in the restaurant, the gym, practice courts, press conferences, hotels, and the treatment room. All of these environments are where the finest details of an athlete's lifestyle are under scrutiny and used to create a perception of the athlete. This perception is a crucial element of LRP. I am certain that what other people or fellow competitors hear and see in the locker room impacts on their perception of an athlete and consequently the athlete's LRP.

A quote from Jose Mourinho (a celebrated football manager who has won two Champion League trophies with Porto FC and Inter Milan, Premiership titles with Chelsea FC, Serie A with Inter Milan and La Liga with Real Madrid) clearly shows his understanding of the importance of LRP and that the locker room is visible anywhere:

"Talking to the media is part of the game. When I go to a press conference before a game, in my mind the game has already started. When I go to a press conference after a game, the game hasn't finished yet. Or if the game is finished, the next one has already started. In a press conference, I am not talking to the people in the room so much as those beyond – my players, other managers, other players, the FA and so on."

All top-flight competitors, coaches and managers know that there is a psychological battle to be won. They instinctively, or through hard earned experience, know when they have to apply pressure to try to gain the upper hand.

Quick points

- **LRP creates an exaggeration of reality.**
- **Other athletes discuss an athlete with LRP positively, which creates an aura of invincibility around the athlete.**
- **The locker room not only refers to the changing room but any place where athletes interact and observe. It is in the restaurant, the gym, practice courts, press conferences, hotels, and the treatment room.**

- CHAPTER 2 -
THE IMPACT OF LOCKER ROOM POWER

"The other athletes played right into Mo's hands and that's a measure of his intimidation factor. No one went out to really test him and he was getting more and more confident. Once he got into the front there was no chance they were coming past him. He was so calm and I am in awe of the way he dominated that race."

Paula Radcliffe's observations on Mo Farah
epitomize Locker Room Power (LRP)

This book will help you learn about the impact of LRP and how you can incorporate it into your game at any level. LRP exists at every level and in every walk of life. Understand it and you create an edge. Awareness gives you a chance to block it from your mind when facing opponents who use LRP to intimidate knowingly or by the nature of their standing in the sport. Bottom line; ignore it and you will be a victim of LRP. Embrace the concept and learn how to create your own LRP.

Your ability to succeed will increase as will your consistency, because others will make your job easier. This chapter highlights a number of world-class athletes who are well aware of this power. I start with Shane Warne, "The greatest spin bowler of all time", and "Warnitude."

Within the game of cricket there have been many world-class bowlers, however none as consistent and destructive as the Australian bowler Shane Warne. Warne put fear in the mind of all who faced him; indeed very few batsmen can walk from the crease having never succumbed to Warne's devilish spin. Gideon Haigh, who wrote the book On Warne, discusses what he labels as 'Warnitude'. As you read this snippet, it will become clear to you that Shane Warne absolutely encompassed Locker Room Power, and what's more, he knew it.

"Batsman after batsman came to the middle determined not to be drawn into the web of Warnitude. They would, they promised themselves, forget the reputation, scorn the aura, and play the ball and not the man. Again and again

they departed remonstrating with themselves that they would do this next time. It seemed unfair, absurd, nearly contrived. Critics carped that Warne got wickets "because he was Shane Warne". Warne's response to this would have been: "Thanks for the compliment." While what Warne was thinking during his little pause was secondary to the complexes forming in the batsman's mind, there was, of course, always something. Mike Tyson once said that he visualised his punches coming out the other side of his opponent's head; I used to feel that Warne did something similar as he stood at the end of his approach, looking at the batsman but also past and through them, as though they were already out. "He gives you the impression that he has already bowled the over to you in his head long before the first delivery comes down," England's Andrew Strauss said of facing him; it was an impression faithful to reality.

© Gideon Haigh 2012 Extracted from On Warne, by Simon and Schuster.

The best way to counter a reputation is to build your own. Once you have created your aura, the impact it can have in the locker room and the surrounding environments an athlete frequents, is vast.

The private moments when preparing for a contest are crucial to a successful performance, because it is during these times that a competitor will buy into his opponent's LRP, become complacent or overconfident about his own LRP, or do what a true competitor does – psyche himself up to play hard from beginning to end whatever the circumstances.

Since we are human, the focus needed to remain in this zone is always subject to attack and penetration. We therefore need tools to deal with a loss of focus so we can still compete almost as effectively, even when this perfect competitive state is breached. It is important to have weapons that can penetrate our opponent's focus, because beating someone who is in the flow is a tough task.

The cliché a big fish in a small pond applies to all budding stars, as everyone begins in a small pond, usually the local club, school or district. What happens to the big fish when he is taken out of his comfort zone? Often the local star is star struck himself when asked to perform at, for example, national level, forgetting or downgrading all his skills and confidence in the face of perceived superior opposition. The athlete effectively throws away any LRP built from earlier success. If, however, he focuses on delivering his skills with the confidence of previous successes, then he can perform against a perceived superior opponent, and much is gained, win or lose. The ability to bring one's skills to any environment is the first sign that an athlete is building a strong mentality for competing. The following examples from swimming show that top performers clearly understand that they have to create an edge and will actively promote their perceived advantage to intimidate, often using the media to get their message across.

The American swimmer Lenny Krayzelburg, quadruple Olympic gold medalist in Sydney 2000, world champion and record holder of 50m, 100m and 200m backstroke, said that he wanted to instil in his rivals the mentality that they were "... racing for second place, and that when it came to major events like the Olympic games, the gold medal was already gone". By saying this to the other swimmers, he was trying to place a very tiny seed of doubt in his competitors' minds, which is all that may be required to get a slight edge over them. These small seeds of doubt can turn into fear, and subconsciously they could find themselves swimming for second place. Small things such as your mental attitude and your body language can influence your competitors' morale - and certainly if you create a reputation for being a strong performer it can make it mighty tough for your competitors mentally.

Australian freestyle swimmer Kieran Perkins, 1992 and 1996 1500m Olympic gold medalist used some powerful mind games to set up an 'aura of invincibility' around his reputation, which seemed to make others feel like they were swimming against a 'legend' instead of just another competitor. Perkins said at the Atlanta Olympics that the mind is so powerful that certain swimmers could actually control the pace of the entire race - he mentioned that when Alex Popov slowed down, the others seemed to slow down as well - almost as if he was orchestrating the whole race!

This is the power a reputation can have, but if you don't have a great reputation yet, don't give anyone else's reputation the time of day and remind yourself that they will only be as good as their play on THAT particular day. It is very unlikely that they will perform as brilliantly as the person you may have seen on TV. Understanding LRP is not only important because you want to build your own, it is also the antidote to the LRP of others. Beware of being the victim of others' reputations and focus on cultivating your own reputation. Don't give your power away. Big name competitors know that ignoring their reputations is easier said than done, which is why it is so important to build your own Locker Room Power.

Quick points

- The best performers in the world understand that they have to create an edge against their opponents. Shane Warne, Serena Williams and Rafael Nadal have worked hard throughout their careers to create and cultivate their edge.

- Players who do not understand LRP tend to get distracted by the power of others. Work hard at not falling into the trap of playing the 'legend' or the guy on TV. Play the person who faces you on the day.

- Remember LRP isn't just created in the pool, on court, in the gym or in practice but also at press conferences, dining areas and anywhere at work where you are watched and analysed.

- CHAPTER 3 -
MY COACHING PHILOSOPHY

"Hard is easy and easy is hard"

Taylor Welch

My expertise is tennis. Few sports examine willpower and the solidity of a person's self-belief as much as tennis. It is hard to find parallels to the lonely and gladiatorial place of a tennis court during a tough match. The 2012 Australian Open final between Novak Djokovic and Rafael Nadal highlighted the complex skills needed to play at the highest level. It was a six-hour test of brutal physical endurance; mental focus and emotional control that delivered accomplished tennis strokes even at the end when fatigue was almost absolute. However, these skills were learned over a long period of time, and although they seem impossible at the start of the journey, in time these abilities become reachable. Understanding my coaching philosophy will help you compete more effectively by inspiring you to learn and trust in the process that will mold you into a mentally tough athlete.

The 'top ten' of my coaching philosophy:

1. Inspiration: Paint the dream.

Excite players by planting the seed that what they want is attainable, and then promptly ask them to forget about it and focus on the immediate achievable goal in front of them. A shift in the excitement needs to happen, an eagerness that fuels the imagination about the possibilities that small improvements can achieve. At any level during a crisis of confidence or poor run of form it is imperative that you find a simple achievable change that will turn things around. The athlete has to believe that when this small change clicks into place results will improve. No matter how competent and knowledgeable coaches are, they are poor coaches if they cannot inspire athletes.

2. Work hard and good things will happen, you just don't know when.

Work to become a better player. Fall in love with the process of small incremental improvements. Searching for the one big thing that will make a significant difference is a red herring. Process over outcome!

3. Success is based on your weapons not your weaknesses. Spend more time building your weapons than improving weaknesses.

Confidence comes from trusting your weapons and over time the belief is so strong that even if you miss four in a row you will still not hesitate on the fifth.

4. Keep it simple. Love the process and never work on more than two things at once.

Less done well is more. Mastering two small improvements that bed in for life is faster than superficially improving six things that are forgotten over time.

5. There is no competitive advantage unless you create it.

Top players create an aura that wins matches before they walk on the court. The locker room is the public domain. How you practice, train, dress, talk, your posture, and the total image you portray, and ultimately your results, determine your Locker Room Power. Anyone can develop Locker Room Power if they show that they are on a mission. Desire is evident and, with the will to work hard, weapons start to emerge and the belief as a competitor begins to shine through. The process of building Locker Room Power begins through understanding what constitutes a competitive mentality.

More coaching tips:

6. Perseverance is the mental foundation.

No individual win makes you good and no individual loss makes you bad. Every player endures. Setbacks are part of the process and are nothing to panic about because each one can be viewed as a confidence builder. You learn that you always get through them and emerge stronger. When a player is really down the choice I give them is "you either carry on or you quit. If you choose to carry on then do it in good spirit and refrain from behaving like it is forced upon you." Each situation has no link to the past unless you create the link. A horror of the past will not be repeated if you take different actions in the present. The magnificence of the future cannot happen without you doing the work in the present.

7. Tone of voice is as or more important than what you say.

This applies to both the coach and the athlete. Use a calm, decisive and firm tone of voice to speak to yourself in your mind or outwardly during matches and practice. Loss of voice control such as becoming high pitched, whining or screaming rarely gets the job done.

8. Feeling sorry for yourself as a competitor is arguably a 'sackable offence'.

When you consider all the suffering and unfairness in the world, athletes who feel sorry for themselves because they cannot get their own way in a sport is an exaggeration of the importance of sport and must be clearly explained. The privilege to be able to take part and compete cannot be lost. I accept this is a learning curve, but the intention is to instil a message that a short period of disappointment after a loss (I recommend one hour) is acceptable, but then it is time to move on and improve again. I know feeling down will still happen in private but you can train it out of people.

I teach this through a simple action. Whenever a player is feeling sorry for himself for the standards required are not met I calmly ask him to leave the court for a minimum of 5 minutes and to come back when he is ready to play. The responsibility is with him to decide when he is ready to return with the required attitude. Players soon learn the standards required to stay on the court. The key here is to behave normally when they return. It requires no explanation or point scoring, just a matter-of-fact attitude from the coach to reincorporate the player seamlessly back into the session.

9. Same shit different level.

What I know as a coach is that the same tests need to be passed at every level. The patience of a coach is to realise that you will repeat the same conversations until you retire from coaching. However, as the player progresses the conversation is at a higher level. The dialogue becomes more sophisticated to help the mind and the game stand up to the pressures of the new level. An athlete realises that at each new level he is getting clearer about how the game is played. For example, a tennis player with a good forehand when ranked at 500 in the world has to improve his forehand further for it to become a good forehand for a ranking of 300, 200 and 100 etc.

10. There is no greater confidence builder than preparation and believing that you are making progress.

This is achieved from a number of areas. A tough physical training block teaches athletes that the 'hard yards' that they once feared can be done. The on-court work, when done with clarity, focus and a sense of fun, teaches the player the ability to switch on and off by working hard then relaxing during a drink's break. The discussions have to be honest, stripping away excuses so that they get used to the harsh environment that is the reality of the sporting world. Yet the player must also believe that they are being armed with the tools to survive and thrive in this harsh environment. I am an educator and as such I need to understand the person so that the correct learning buttons can be pressed. It is imperative that I help them to understand themselves so that they can gain the confidence that comes from being aware of their areas of fragility and recognising and using the newfound strengths they have gained in their tennis minds.

- CHAPTER 4 -
COMPETITIVE MENTALITY

"If you even dream of beating me you'd better wake up and apologise."

Muhammad Ali

A competitive mentality is a state of mind. Developing the mind of a champion takes time and experience. It takes years of repetition, with current research indicating it takes "10,000 hours" to perfect the skills and gain the wisdom to compete at the highest level. The athlete will reflect on disappointing losses, steadily improving the discipline and control of his thoughts under pressure to create the mentality of a champion. Star performers cultivate a competitive desire for success that becomes instinctive.

How do they attain this state of mind and train their minds to stay in the present? They need to be aware of expectations and learn to manage them effectively. For example in tennis a player faced with a big point in a match can view it as a point that may win or lose him the match. Unless it is match point this is not true. This creates extra pressure on the point. Depending on the result of the point the player can lose focus by being too happy or too disappointed.

If a good match is won the player's mind can stretch to thinking he can win the tournament and if he wins the tournament then his ranking will rise and that will impact his career. The problem is, in his next match when faced with a big point, that point represents not only the match, but possibly the tournament and his career. No wonder the player chokes – who wants to play one point for their career?

Once aware of the devious 'mind stretch', you can and must monitor what you are thinking in key moments and keep bringing yourself back to the fact that it is only one point and represents nothing more. It is a cliché and sounds boring but it is about building your career literally one point at a time.

This is vitally important when developing a competitive mentality. The key to a winning mind-set in all competition is the discipline to control excess emotion, to stay in the present and to remain focused on the job. If things are going well and you let your mind drift, focus on the present task is lost. When you are winning, it is tempting to project forward into the future, imagining all the wonderful things that will come with victory. However, victory may not ensue if your mind is not fully present in the match. When your mind wanders you can begin thinking of what may or may not happen, such as who is watching, what your ranking will be when you win etc. Understand a fundamental problem: if your mind is distracted and not in the present, there is no-one mentally there to play for you in your absence!

When your mind returns to the present, it is often to a vastly different place (with a different score) to the one you left. Panic sets in. This can easily lead to another mental error, which is falling into a state of regret for failing to capitalize on a winning position. In these circumstances it is easy for the mind to jump into the immediate past or into a negative future ("I'm never going to win, I've totally blown it" or "What will everyone say if I lose?") Yet only minutes earlier the situation seemed so rosy.

If you slip into the past and think of all the opportunities you blew in this and other matches, again you are not fully present in the current match. You cannot play properly when you are not fully focused on the present. Players repeatedly invite the same result again and again because they cannot discipline their mind to remain in the present.

When you slip into the past or project yourself into the future you will attach the emotions of that time to your actions of the present. The baggage of these emotions is detrimental to achieving peak performance in the present.

> *"If you do what you've always done, you'll get what you've always gotten."*
>
> Anthony Robbins

Another key to being a brilliant competitor is the understanding that you often need to unsettle your opponent's mind rather than try to defeat their game. Champions read people well; they constantly monitor their opponents' reactions and moods to find a way of using pressure to erode their confidence.

There is a strong element of poker in sport. One of the finest examples of this was the wonderful Rumble in the Jungle where Muhammad Ali, who was past his best, fought George Foreman, a boxer in his prime and full of confidence. Foreman was the better boxer at that particular point in their careers and was hot favourite. However, Ali had other ideas – a plan that attacked Foreman's mind and a strategy that turned the fight into a personal contest rather than a pure boxing match.

The rope-a-dope tactic employed by Ali, (he shielded his face with his gloves and leaned back on the ropes allowing Foreman to hit him repeatedly), worked because it was unexpected. (Ali had always prided himself on his speed). Ali talked non-stop during the fight, taunting Foreman into a fury by constantly asking him after each hammer blow that Foreman landed: "Is that all you got? I thought they said you had the hardest punch ever. Is that your best?" Foreman's anger and desire to use his superior power clouded his judgment and his ability to listen to his corner. He tried to hurt Ali badly; to shut him up. And in the process proceeded to punch himself into exhaustion. At this point Ali attacked and knocked him out! Ali had found the key to beating the person, not the boxer.

The contest was not about boxing; it was about one man unsettling another's mental equilibrium. It is important to understand that for this tactic to work Ali had to know himself and have total faith that he was brave and strong enough to take the punishment, a sustained beating, without losing his discipline or his clarity of mind during the painful seven or more rounds it would take for Foreman to tire.

Quick Points

- **Stay in the present.**
- **Monitor your opponent's reactions and body language.**
- **Try to unsettle your opponent, make the experience uncomfortable for them.**
- **You can beat the person rather than their game if you find a way to get under their skin.**

- CHAPTER 5 -
PLAY TO GAIN

"You just try to play tough and focus point for point. Sounds so boring, but it's the right thing to do out there."

Rafael Nadal

Rafael Nadal is a fantastic competitor. If you listen to his interviews he always speaks about working hard every day to improve. He plays each point with ferocious intensity yet moves onto the next point without any baggage.

When faced with a 5th set in the 2008 Wimbledon final, having already lost a two sets to love lead and squandering two match points, he was asked how he overcame the disappointment.

"Disappointment! Are you crazy! When all my life I dream of winning Wimbledon and still the opportunity is so big? I only have one set to win! I focus to hold my serve and I know if I can hold my serve then when we are maybe 3-3 Roger must know he must beat me and this is difficult, no?"

Nadal always looks at what he can gain. He plays to gain a Wimbledon title. He never thinks about what he has to lose; only what he has to gain.

How does one acquire this mentality? A useful analogy you can use to achieve this mentality is to develop an attitude of PLAY TO GAIN.

Visualize a ladder that you have to climb that is fixed to the side of a 250-metre skyscraper. There is a resting platform every 30 metres. Imagine that each match you play equates to one rung on the ladder. If you lose a match you remain in the same place – you lose nothing. Likewise with each set, game or point. As long as your goal is to improve then you can only go up the ladder. Every lost match simply means you have to keep working to improve so that you can gain a rung on the ladder. You can only gain a point, game, set or match. The consequences of not winning are simply staying where you are on the ladder. I repeat: you lose nothing.

The first thing most people would do is look up at the ladder and the building to see how far and large the task will be. You see the goal. This in itself is daunting, so sensibly you decide to focus on a process goal, which is climb to the first 30 metre-resting platform.

At the start you are fresh and there is very little outside pressure. The height is not yet a problem. In fact after 10-15 metres you can enjoy the view and even a bit of wind is hardly noticed or even welcome. Players with ability and good coaching tend to progress quickly at the lower levels and climbing is mostly fun.

As you climb higher up the ladder, looking around too much causes problems. You begin to compare yourself to other players and how far they are up their ladders. You notice the wind and worry how it will feel higher up. The ground starts to seem a long way down. If your arms and legs feel a bit tired you wonder if you are strong enough. You may begin to feel isolated as friends get left behind. The solution is to narrow your focus on the next rung and nothing else until you've reached your target platform where you can take stock and fuel yourself for the next phase.

Imagine you are connected to your coach and the world at large through an earpiece. This can be tuned into any frequency, allowing you to listen to anyone you choose. As you get up to around 150 metres the method of coaching becomes increasingly important and your discipline becomes crucial to your success. Your coach needs to help you understand the choices and distractions, and encourage you to focus on improving, encourage you to always work until you are capable of climbing up the next rung. Whatever the score, the most productive action is to do everything you can to gain the next point. If you gain enough points you gain a game and so on. There is little value in concentrating on how long you have been stuck on the same rung, because as long as you want to go forward (up) the job is to get better and stronger until you can climb up to the next rung. Your team has to help you understand that every player faces powerful obstacles that sow seeds of doubt, maybe so strong as to persuade you to quit and go back down the ladder or settle at one of the resting places along the way.

Do not fear or worry about other players who seem to be climbing easier and faster than you. Remember, progression is personal and quick progress does not mean it will continue at the same rate. The rare exceptional talent who may reach dizzy heights quickly only to slow near the top is not your concern. Your target is not people. It is your ladder and if your goal is to be

No. 1 in the world or to become club champion, it is your ladder to climb. You climb poorly when you do not concentrate fully on your own ladder and gain a good rhythm, whether it is with the speed of a tortoise or a hare.

Wind and rain will slow you down and make certain times miserable, cold, and lonely. The slippery ladder can be scary as hell, but persevere because the sun always returns.

Success can also cause fear of heights to kick in. 200 metres up can be very uncomfortable, especially when you look down. It can be a lonely place because you know few people and some of the people around you might seem unfriendly; they may be wary of you, the new guy or girl gate-crashing their party. They will test your resolve to stay with them. Again the best answer is to work hard and keep focused on your climb.

The higher you get the greater the choice of earpiece frequency and with this comes the responsibility to choose wisely. Who do you tune into?

There are undoubtedly negative personalities on this journey up the ladder who will voice their doubts. Ironically this could be friends, a coach, or parents. In fact this could be anyone who tells you or by their actions implies that you have reached your potential; that the target is too high or that it's only other people with incredible luck or more talent who can climb to the top. There are many who deliberately or inadvertently weaken your resolve by highlighting all the reasons why you can't make it. Avoid anyone who encourages you to stop, to enjoy the view, to forget about the next platform up or try to limit you to the level of his or her ambition.

The person can be close to you, such as a girlfriend, boyfriend, or significant other who may resent the time apart or the time spent practicing. They may feel second in priority. They might fear losing you if you climb too high, to a place where your choices widen. Apart from an odd glance there is no need to look down, to the side, or up between stages. When you reach a rest area, enjoy the moment, replenish your strength, evaluate the next goal and without hanging around too long start the climb again, eyes firmly fixed on the next rung. Even the greatest players struggle if their lives become complicated. It is extremely difficult to compete effectively if there are too many distractions.

Tiger Woods is an example of a dominant force whose ability to perform was weakened due to huge disruptions in his private life. Former coach Butch Harmon said at the time that Woods looked lost and was playing the worst he had ever seen him play. "He had to get his head right; get his life in order before he could even think about playing golf."

After significant success you will invariably be approached by sycophants who will tell you that you have made it, that the rest of the climb will be easy, that you can do other things and that your current support team may not appreciate the depth of your talent. They suggest changes by implying that although your team has done a great job, you have probably outgrown their abilities. The undermining message is that they are in the know and can guide you to the big time with inner secrets.

A worse situation is, if the team around you become intoxicated by the heights and join in with the self-congratulations and distractions, no longer grounding and guiding you, fueling unrealistic expectations rather than a desire to work even harder to climb the last few rungs. Do not underestimate the complexity of success and the careful thought and evaluation needed in choosing your team.

The top of the building is a wonderful achievement. However, many a successful person will tell you that although the view is fantastic and rewarding, quickly you notice there is a bridge you can cross to a larger tower. Then you have to decide whether to attempt to climb again, because if you don't someone else most certainly will. The unwavering focus and ability to keep improving is the key to reaching and remaining at high levels.

It is far easier to continue to climb if you tune into the encouraging voices that support you, understand your aspirations and firmly yet gently push you to consistently improve. All that is needed is focused effort and the discipline to block destructive voices.

Play To Gain

Keep it simple with one objective in mind – gain the next point, the next game, the next set, and the next match.

Quick points

- **You lose nothing.** In reality, what actually changes in your life if you lose a match? If you lose you end up in the same place that you began!
- **Focus on your own ladder.** No-one knows how high their ladder will be, but keep climbing until you have reached your limit.
- **You gain.** However high you climb you will be a stronger person with a better view than those who don't.
- **Find your limits.** Even if you choose to go down the ladder you have lost nothing. At least you have learned how high you were prepared to climb, or how high you were able to climb, and have experienced a higher perspective than that of ground level.
- **Choose the team around you wisely.**

- CHAPTER 6 -
WEAPONS

"Enter every activity without giving mental recognition to the possibility of defeat. Concentrate on your strengths, instead of your weaknesses... on your powers, instead of your problems."

Paul J Meyer

I believe that athletes need to develop a minimum of two weapons, as well as a strong mind, to really hurt opponents. Attributes that strike fear into opponents' minds and have the power to unnerve opponents. Many gifted athletes in sport have more than two weapons and this simply means they have more choice.

Great players are remembered for their weapons. A significant attribute is their ability to use them in key moments. Interestingly, Babe Ruth (American baseball legend) is remembered for his home runs, yet he also had the record for the most strikeouts. Meanwhile, Michael Jordan holds two records: the first for the most game-winning baskets and the second for the most misses in a game-winning last basket situation.

"I have missed more than 9,000 shots in my career. I have lost almost 300 games. On 26 occasions I have been entrusted to take the game winning shot... and I missed. I have failed over and over and over again in my life. And that's precisely why I succeed."

Michael Jordan

Under pressure, the best competitors are always ready to step up to the plate and use their weapons. This means they have the most practice and experience in tough situations. They have gathered enough self-belief to be able to go for their shots. However, they are also sensible enough to remain optimistic when they fail. They understand through experience that in tight moments they have a better than average chance of winning. This is because they have a history of backing themselves in the moment.

Everyone is vulnerable. We all have a weakness, an Achilles' heel, yet champions are remembered for their weapons, not their weaknesses. If their weaknesses far exceed their weapons, they will not become champions. If their weaknesses are so great that they break down before they can use their weapons, then these exposed areas will have to be improved. Weapons are the key to winning. Any limitations or weaknesses only need to be good enough to keep you in the game long enough to use your weapons.

In an interview I conducted with Tim Henman, I asked Tim about his weapons and his awareness of them.

> *"Yes. I knew my attacking style would hurt opponents and I worked hard at perfecting my approaches and volleys. Disappointingly, for a major part of my career I never classed my athletic ability and balance as a weapon, having always been told that I was the small skinny guy who needed to get stronger. Late in my career Larry Stefanki emphasised this weapon and when I thought about it I realised he was right – I was a great athlete, fast and balanced. It would have been a help to have known this earlier."*

Many players may struggle to identify their weapons. With regard to tennis, a weapon is considered to be a shot that wins you the majority of your points. Most tennis players have big serves or forehands. As stated before, I believe that an athlete should have a minimum of two weapons. If you consider your serve and forehand to be your weaponry then you should be aware of this and be prepared to utilize them fully in your matches.

When I work with players who find weapon identification troublesome I simply ask them to list two possible weapons and decide if these are good enough to achieve the goal they have set. If the answer is yes then I ask them to list two weaknesses. I explain that it is the contrast between their strengths and weaknesses that make them unique, but it is their strengths that will help them achieve their goals. I get them to center on a mind-set that focuses on their opponents having to deal with the weapons they can deliver. I encourage them to use their strengths proactively to ask difficult questions of their opponents. If they lose, it will be evident what weaknesses or strengths need to improve. This is a great positive because it is a simple and realistic way of setting practice goals.

It is imperative that losses do not affect the mind-set and that the athlete continues to work at building his weapons. He must always have respect for his own strengths. His mind-set must remain clear that the message is to force opponents to deal with their weapons. As part of this process the coach has to plan the competition schedule carefully so the level is challenging. However, it must still be within a zone where the athlete can be successful; where they can employ these weapons and still have the opportunity to improve and hone them. The subtle change from a reactive mind-set to a proactive mind-set that focuses on what weapons the athlete can deliver is a key turning point.

*"I let my racket do the talking. That's what I am all about, really.
I just go out and win tennis matches"*

Pete Sampras

The most impressive form of attack is to use your own weapons. These are your most practiced and therefore most trusted ways to create fear or doubt in your opponent's mind. If, for instance, your best weapon is your forehand drive, hit a big shot with it as soon as possible in the match. This will make a positive statement to yourself and to your opponent. Effectively you are saying, "I'm going to put you under pressure with my forehand". This not only makes you feel confident but may also have the added advantage of sparking off fearful thoughts in the mind of the opponent such as, "If I'm going to hit to his forehand it's going to have to be a great shot, otherwise he'll take the point".

Even if you miss the forehand, you can still make a positive statement. For instance, you can convey the message, "Ok, I missed this time but be careful hitting to my forehand, I'm not always going to miss those shots". Similarly your opponent may think: "I was lucky he missed that – his forehand looks like a lethal weapon". The statements you make in a match should be planned and deliberate, and are as powerful as the intent and commitment with which they are delivered.

Quick points

- Evaluate your key weapons. (These may be mental, tactical or physical).

- Identify the weapons that you need to improve.

- Try to eliminate a real weakness in your game if it prevents you from using your chosen weapons.

- Reassess your weapons at appropriate times to increase confidence and refuel your desire to improve further.

- Plan how you are going to make statements of intent so that you are prepared before you go on court.

- CHAPTER 7 -
PSYCHOLOGICAL STATEMENTS

"The fact that we are human means that even the best competitors can be 'rocked' by a true statement of intent."

David Sammel

If the above statement were a fallacy there would never be upsets in sport. There are many athletes who are arguably less talented than some of their peers, yet are able to beat them. Rafael Nadal has a winning record against Roger Federer, who is arguably equal to or better than Nadal in many areas of the game. It is Nadal's level of intent behind his aggression that can and has caused Federer problems. Nadal plays with a ferocious commitment to win that unsettles most opponents.

The purpose of a statement is to deliver a clear message of intent to your opponent. If you understand the power and importance of making a statement then you begin to recognize the art of winning the mental game. Making statements and building Locker Room Power is critical to your success.

Apart from boxing, tennis is possibly the most difficult and mentally aggressive of all sports. Many people allude to the fact that tennis players are modern-day gladiators. Certainly the best players in the world understand mental strength and the ability to make an opponent feel uncomfortable.

If you are being outplayed and are finding it difficult to impose your game on your opponent, you need to find something to attack. My advice is to anticipate an opponent's weapon and make it a mission to counterattack off their weapon.

It is human nature to think twice when your previously impregnable onslaught is breached powerfully. Churchill did not win World War II by deciding to bomb Berlin early in the conflict, but by doing so it caused Hitler to be irritated and change German tactics from bombing the airfields to launching a vicious bombardment of British cities. This effectively allowed Britain into the game. It gave British planes time to get into the air and defend the skies.

Psychological Statements

When defending a poor position against an onslaught, you must find something to attack! It just might become a turning point and shows your opponent that you are not meekly accepting the battering.

In a closely fought contest momentum will ebb and flow. A very powerful statement is the ability to absorb punishment with a clear mind. As admirable as fighting and scrambling are, they are not effective unless you fight with the clear intention to seize any chance to deliver a statement with the absolute message, "I might be struggling but I still can find a way to hurt you in the battle!"

This fighting quality, coupled with an alertness to turn things around actually allows you to see an opportunity when under pressure. Often I have seen a player defending desperately without ever planning a counterattack. Anticipate one move ahead and try to use this early anticipation to attack the opponent's weapon with total commitment.

It is important to understand where you are in the world of competition and, in doing so, use each match as a test of how good you are, how good your opponent is and what you need to learn if you are to accomplish your goals. Napoleon Hill confirms this succinctly in the quote: "Do not wait; the time will never be 'just right'. Start where you stand, and work with whatever tools you may have at your command, and better tools will be found as you go along."

Hill is also saying that if you do your best with what you have on the day, you will learn faster than if you shy away from competing. There is no way of avoiding loss. Everyone loses. However, win or lose, it is the quality of your attitude and strategies you employ during the loss that your opponent will remember. What positive energy did you bring to the table that will be respected no matter what the outcome? Even during a rout, try to create something that you can build on, something that momentarily stuns your opponent. These statements of intent may pay dividends years later when your skills are more competitive and you are in a real fight with the same opponent. If you repeat a blow made years earlier your opponent will remember this, and the respect for your attitude when you were less competitive will count volumes in the current encounter. This could create the slight hesitation in your opponent that could swing the balance of power and allow you to seize the day.

Recognising that a statement has unnerved an opponent is the key to learning how to unlock opponents as people. Often it is one tactic or one blow that knocks their confidence. Be alert to notice the hurt or fear, and then probe to discover if it is a temporary or a real issue for them. It is during these moments that you should work and focus hardest to take the match from them or, at the very least, shift some impetus and momentum back in your favour.

> *"Hold serve, Hold serve, Hold serve. Focus, Focus, Focus. Be confident, be confident, be confident. Hold serve. Hold, Hold, Hold. Move Up, Attack, Kill. Smile. Hold!!!"*
>
> Serena Williams

The cycle of tough competition is summarized in Figure 1.

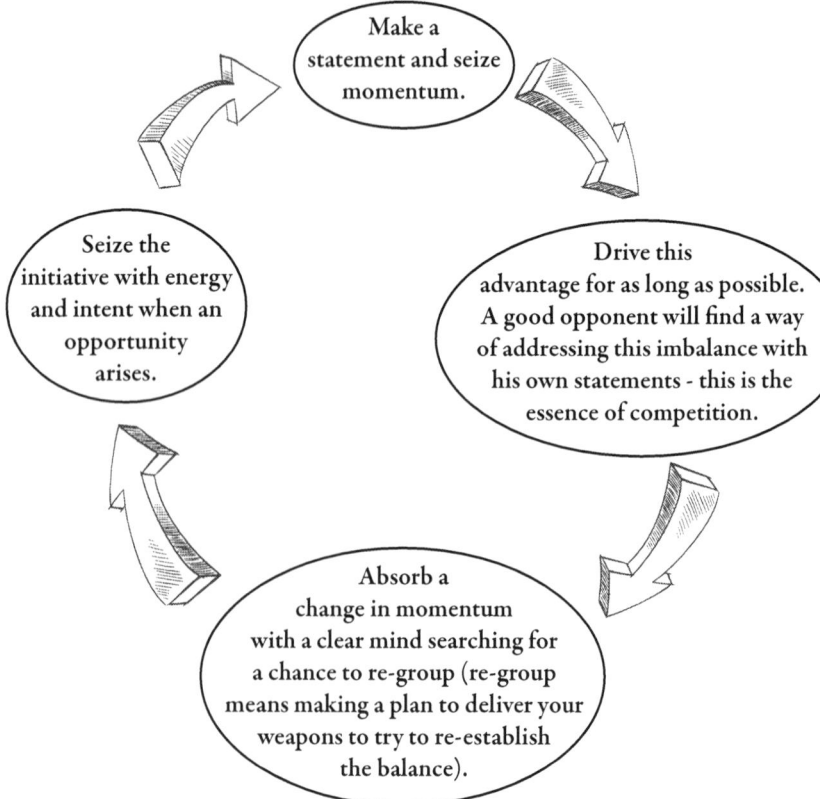

Psychological Statements

This cycle can occur countless times in a match and actually sometimes occurs within individual points, within a game, or at various times during a set.

> *"You cannot deliver statements in a match at the right time if you do not plan to do so."*
>
> David Sammel

We all know that at every level the one thing that separates those who win consistently from those who do not is the mental game. Yet, amazingly, if you ask players the last time they practiced their mental approach to the game (e.g. actually visualizing different situations and how they would deal with them), most would struggle to remember. In contrast, if you also asked them the last time they practiced a backhand or a serve, they could quickly recall. You will not be able to deliver statements in a match at the right time consistently if you do not plan to do so. Equally you have to be confident in your abilities to deliver a statement. Serving and volleying the first point, when you have not practiced this combination of shots, will be delivered in hope rather than intent, and if it works will be interpreted as lucky by you and probably the same by your opponent. Luck is not something to be feared.

My experience on the tennis tour has taught me that it makes a huge difference to a match when a player goes on to the court knowing the exact statements he will make against an opponent. Find out what it can do for you.

Quick points

- **Making a statement using a weapon can have a powerful mental impact on your opponent.**
- **Plan how you are going to deliver your own statements and respond to statements delivered by your opponent.**

- CHAPTER 8 -
INTIMIDATION AND GAMESMANSHIP

"In the semi-finals, I faced Federer, and it is true that I felt plethoric on clay... as true as the match seemed intimidating, I felt respect. I am not saying fear. Never."

Rafael Nadal

Intimidation is part of the game. This should not be confused with gamesmanship, which is the use of actions not associated with playing the game. Most good players do not need to use, nor do they condone, gamesmanship. However, these athletes will have a plan to combat it if they find themselves on the receiving end of it. Intimidation comes in various forms. It is not only the actions of other players that can intimidate, but also venues. Many players fail to perform at their best the first time they play at Wimbledon, intimidated and overwhelmed by the history, the enormity of their achievement to get there and the sheer size of the event and the crowds. Here is a story of Arvind Parmar who was initially intimidated by Wimbledon rather than the seeded player he was about to face.

Some may think that 'ignorance is bliss', but not in sport. Arvind Parmar qualified for Wimbledon in 1999, winning three good matches, including a victory over Max Mirnyi (Belarus) in the final round in four sets. He was confident and ready to take on the 25th seed Alberto Costa (French Open Champion 2002) in the 1st round, and seemingly relaxed for his debut at the world's biggest tournament. The match was called and as we walked from the locker room towards Court 13, I noticed the blood drain from his face. The enormity of the occasion, plus the realization that he was achieving the childhood dream of playing at Wimbledon, hit him hard. I had a minute to give him something to hang onto or he would be history, unable to use the confidence he had gained in the qualifying rounds. I grabbed him by the shoulders and said firmly, "Arvind look at me! Remember this! Five sets is a long time. I know you didn't expect to feel this way and you are suddenly sh$%ing yourself but that's okay. I promise you even if you lose the first two sets, you will play. And when you do play, you will play well. Remember five

Intimidation and Gamesmanship

sets is a long time, so don't panic – you will settle down and play."

I expected him to struggle early but was not prepared for how quickly he would be 0-6, 0-3 down. He held serve for 1-3, then found some form and broke serve. He went on to win 0-6, 7-6(4), 6-3, 6-3. He said after the match that all he thought about whilst paralysed with nerves was "five sets is a long time – the game will come". And once he connected with a couple of good returns he was on his way. What I learnt from this is that players often ignore their feelings or are unaware of what is ahead, hoping that miraculously everything will fall into place.

Leaving mental issues to chance is generally unsuccessful, whereas picturing what is ahead enables the player to anticipate and deal with their fears or insecurities. This picturing in itself alleviates apprehension and helps players to combat these feelings and change their perspective on the situation. Arvind battled his nerves, and once he relaxed his form shone through for an upset victory [when a low ranked player beats a seeded player].

Arvind was confident in his game, but mistakenly believed in the lead up that he was totally at ease and comfortable to be playing Wimbledon on a show court, seeming relaxed through every one of our pre-match discussions. He had not accepted the possibility that nerves and stage fright might occur and that this is normal, which is the last minute message I fortunately managed to impart on the walk to the court. He had to have something to hold onto, to see himself coping and overcoming the paralysis that suddenly struck.

When players honestly deal with issues before they step out to perform, then they acquire the consistency every competitor craves, since the surprises only come from external events, not from within.

Another common reaction to feeling intimidated is for players to psyche themselves up into a frenzy of anger and aggression in order to overcome the fear. They then take this aggression to the field or court and blindly attack the opponent with rash tackles, over-aggressive shot making or picking a fight. This approach can gain some success if it intimidates or temporarily rushes an opponent, but success is random and unassured because experienced opponents will weather the early storm and capitalize on the rash errors and the drop in energy when the initial adrenalin rush subsides.

In the real world of competition you will at times encounter gamesmanship and must be prepared to deal with it. If not, you will almost certainly fall victim to letting an opponent's poor or desperate antics divert your attention or annoy you to the extent that you lose the match. If you recognize that gamesmanship is being used to distract you, you can begin to deal with it, putting into action your own plan. Retaliating with gamesmanship is an option, but responding positively to such situations by making a statement is more powerful.

The following story is an example of an event that may or may not have involved gamesmanship but nevertheless needed to be addressed by the player whose mind and game was disrupted.

In the 2005 US Open semi-final between Mary Pierce and Elena Dementieva, Pierce took a 12-minute injury time-out after losing the first set. During the time-out, Mary re-grouped and Elena lost her rhythm, complaining after the match that effectively this was gamesmanship on Mary's part.

Although the break had bothered her, Elena did nothing to re-group her mind or put pressure on Mary whilst she was lying face down on the court for back treatment. For instance, had she stood close to Mary and questioned the umpire as to how much injury time was being made available, not only may it have alleviated some of her own stress, but Mary would have felt her proximity and she and the trainer may have felt obliged to be quicker. Certainly it would have distracted her otherwise undisturbed massage and thinking time.

Whether or not Mary's action was deliberate, the fact is it got under Elena's skin and she did nothing about it. As with any situation in tennis, there is no guarantee that making a statement in retaliation to an opponent's actions or gamesmanship will change the result. But it could, and competing is about doing everything possible within the rules to win. If the break had not bothered Elena then staying relaxed and doing nothing in retaliation would have been the right thing to do.

Dealing with players' perceived or real statements of intent improves with experience. As a coach I believe we have a duty to our players to help them become aware of certain statements they can make to unsettle opponents.

Intimidation and Gamesmanship

However, this must not be confused with advocating gamesmanship. Apart from being ethically unacceptable, gamesmanship can often stir up some startling emotions that can backfire on a player. A crowd will not usually appreciate gamesmanship and the response (i.e. booing the bad guy and cheering for the good guy) can unnerve the perpetrator and/or lift the game of the player on the receiving end.

Quick points

- It is appropriate to respect opponents. However, as Nadal says, "Fear - never."

- Have a strategy to deal with nerves and potentially intimidating situations.

- Do not use gamesmanship but have a plan ready in case you have to deal with it.

- CHAPTER 9 -
PERSONALITY USED AS A WEAPON

"Sports do not build character. They reveal it."
Heywood Broun

It is advantageous in a match to set the scene early before your opponent has settled down. Plan to show your opponent your intent from the first point. Use your most effective statements in your own particular game that sit right with your personality. This congruency is of great importance because you can only be truly committed to something if you totally believe in what you are doing – something that is part of you as a person and thus as a competitor. Establish key phrases to say to yourself, and key actions to take that encourage you, to deliver messages that highlight your competitive personality.

You also have to take into account the competitive personality of the opponent. It would be foolish to be ultra-aggressive in manner when competing against a player like Lleyton Hewitt. By deliberately trying to intimidate him you could easily stir his competitive fire and create a problem for yourself. Another example of a foolish use of showing off was during a 1st round match in the 2008 Monte Carlo Open. Ramirez-Hidalgo was leading Federer 5-1 in the third set when he played a winner between his legs. He proceeded to celebrate and play to the crowd to such an extent that it bordered on disrespectful to the talents of perhaps the greatest player of all time. Federer, duly annoyed, woke up and taught him a lesson by winning 7-6 in the third.

Remember, whilst the statements you make are important, choosing when to make a statement requires a competitive feel that is incredibly powerful. You have to take into account your personality as a player and that of your opponent. John McEnroe would have been useless trying to be as cool and collected as Björn Borg, yet it is important to remember that by his own admission, he played his best tennis against Borg when he remained calm, sticking to mostly positive statements rather than resorting to the negative.

This is because he quickly learned that whatever he did on his side of the court had no effect on Borg, so gamesmanship and histrionics gained him no advantage.

McEnroe knew he had to beat Borg with his tennis. This challenge was irresistible. It became a source of great pleasure and helped develop his well-known respect for Borg. He felt that controlling his personality on court was a sign of his respect for Borg, who was the person he most needed to respect him as a player and a person. Had he acted disrespectfully when playing Borg, he would never have earned the high opinion of this living legend. Because McEnroe had little admiration for the talents of most other players, he often used negative behaviour to influence the match if he felt in danger of losing to someone with less talent. He struggled to find the discipline to temper the excesses of his emotions. However, against Borg, he was able to control his emotions, which was the key to him producing his best tennis. This is why he was so deeply affected by Borg's early retirement.

Sir Alex Ferguson, the most successful football manager in British history, has often used the media to deliver messages to test the resolve or mental strength of opposing managers. Here is a typical statement to increase pressure on an opponent: "If Chelsea drop points, the cat's out in the open. And you know what cats are like – sometimes they don't come home."

Andy Murray is another example of a player using a TV interview to deliver a positive message: *"I'm not planning on getting caught up in the whole hype and, you know, the pressure and whatnot, because I don't think that that helps if you do. I'm going to try and concentrate on playing and winning matches. You can let the pressure affect you if you want to. You can let the expectation get to you if you really want to, but I'm just going to play tennis and not worry about the rest of the stuff, because I don't think it's good for your game."* Official press conference after the AEGON Tournament at Queens' Club, 2009.

It is interesting that Murray says "You can let the pressure affect you if you want to." This shows us that he sees pressure and the way you deal with it as a choice, and is telling the tennis world the choice he makes!

In summary, the best competitors in the world have found a way to tune their personalities into working effectively for them under pressure. They have disciplined themselves to use the strengths of their personalities and temper the weaknesses or excesses that hurt their performance. They are also very astute in how they demonstrate their personality strengths by using various actions and statements to deliver their overall message.

Quick points

- Identify your personality type on and off court.
- Let your opponent know you are competitive - this may be in a cool subtle way or a louder, more obvious way depending on your nature.
- Be aware of your opponent's personality - then you can decide the best course of action to combat it.

CHAPTER 10

UPSIDE DOWN – IS YOUR WEAKNESS A STRENGTH?

"A genius in the wrong position could look like a fool"

Idowu Koyenikan,

This story is about how your weaknesses define you as much as your strengths and it's about a Wimbledon champion, Richard Krajicek, who was a young player at the club in Holland where I was a player/coach, my very first coaching job. I played alongside him on one of the teams and ran the team coaching sessions, but I was not his individual coach. He was part of the Dutch Federation and he had an individual coach. As a top junior he had a very good game and a two-handed backhand. His private coach decided that he was physically too slow to have a two-handed backhand, which didn't quite make sense to me and decided to change him to a one-handed backhand and this backhand was terrible. I argued tooth and nail against it, but I lost the argument and Richard went on to eventually win Wimbledon.

We had a coffee at Wimbledon a few years after that and I said to him, "I'm intrigued Richard. What do you think would happened to your career if you'd stuck with the two-handed backhand? It was a really good shot and your single-handed backhand obviously got better but it was never a strength, it was always a weakness. I argued against the change and I've always wondered what you think would have happened if you had stuck to the two-hander, especially for return to serve."

The answer he gave me floored me. He said, "I don't think I'd ever have won Wimbledon. In fact, I probably would've been a top 30 player. I don't think I would have been a top 10, top five player. I actually made number two in the world."

I said, "Why is that?"

He said, "Well, you were right. My two-hander was so much better than my one-hander but when I changed to a one-handed backhand, something changed in me because it was so bad. I suddenly had a very simple method of play because I still wanted to win. I had to serve and volley, I had to get to the net as soon as possible because I couldn't rally off the baseline like I could off the two-handed backhand. I used the slice backhand, which you know I had already, to get to the net as soon as possible and it made tennis very clear for me. I had one way of playing and I had to get forward because there's no way I could play on the baseline."

"The game became so simple, my serve got so much better because I had to serve and volley, my chip charge got so much better and I became a total attacking player, which, you know, I hadn't been. Although it was never a good shot, I believe it's the reason why I won Wimbledon."

Suddenly a scary thought dawned on me ... "Wow, I could've messed up the chance of a Wimbledon champion." The thing that clicked in my head is that as individuals, it's about the total package. What do you bring to the table as a total package? And your weaknesses actually define you as much as your strengths.

The other thing that came from that is, if you embrace your weaknesses as part of you, the contrast is incredibly powerful because if somebody has a weakness which is not so weak that you just can't do anything with it and you can sometimes produce good results off that weakness, that unsettles opponents because it creates doubt. It is difficult to a) break your own patterns to target a weakness and b) harder psychologically if you get burnt by that weakness.

In sport, it's not always about whether you get hurt or not, it's about when you get hurt. If you target a weakness in a big moment and the weakness suddenly isn't there, that is very destabilising for opponents. The bottom line is, you need to embrace your weaknesses in life because they help define you as a person and understand how managing your package of strengths and weaknesses is very, very powerful. The key is that Richard saw his weakness as a major weapon – the reason why he was so good which is a fantastic example of turning a negative not only into a positive but into a weapon.

In my own life I know my size and appearance can be daunting which is a strength in many circumstances but in different situations where an automatic friendliness is helpful this strength is a weakness. Through mental preparation I can manage how I approach people, which is why self-awareness is a helpful tool in helping us understand how our strengths and weaknesses impact others.

Quick points

- Strengths and weaknesses define who you are as a person. They are also situational so therefore a strength can be a weakness and vice versa.
- Defining your strengths and weaknesses helps you develop an effective package which can make tactics very simple.
- Self-awareness is helpful in managing how we use our strengths and weaknesses to impact others and ourselves.

- CHAPTER 11 -
RADIATORS – POSITIVE ENERGY SOURCES

"Enthusiasm is the mother of effort, and without it nothing great was ever achieved."

Ralph Waldo Emerson

The greatest energy source in the world is enthusiasm. It is purely positive and essential to success. It is powerful, healthy and infectious, bringing joy to the work we undertake. When people learn to tap into enthusiasm (often referred to in terms of passion, love of the game, great work ethic and attitude) there is an amazing amount of effortless energy to burn. Enthusiastic people only need to ensure they get enough rest to recharge the batteries and off they go again, completely refreshed, even after setbacks.

The greatest exponents of enthusiastic energy are young children. They will partake in any activity they think is fun with great joy and energy. The killer of enthusiasm is often poor coaching that deflates the enthusiasm in athletes. This applies equally to children and adults. A coach or teacher has a responsibility to be imaginative, creating interesting and engaging ways of practicing and learning.

It is clear that succeeding in anything has its element of grind. Sometimes the hard work is fun, but at other times it is not and just has to be done. Time management is crucial in achieving the right balance to progress – overload a person with grind and there is danger of killing enthusiasm; not enough grind and repetition then the skills needed are not embedded strongly enough to excel. This is a big part to the art of coaching.

As children become teenagers, their workload increases and the skill required to manage their time becomes more complex. The overall feeling is still that the work should be fun, but now must also include the awareness that the work is worthwhile. Young hopefuls need to believe that delayed reward is worth it and that achieving their goals will feel so good that it fuels their enthusiasm. During this phase of their development, the key is to manage the level of competition and the setting of goals as effectively as possible to sustain their enthusiasm.

This process of planning the right level of competition and setting appropriate goals is not easy to manage. Therefore, most young competitors need a support team. This team should have the skills and knowledge to manage the process successfully and foster enthusiasm for the task. If this process is not managed well, competitors will begin to draw on other energy sources, namely anger or fear, to drive them forwards. Unfortunately, these are negative energy sources, which not only destroy promising careers but also sap the energy levels of those around them.

Quick points

- Enthusiasm is hands down the best energy source.
- If you love the hard work, understand the necessity of the 'grind' and are prepared to get up the morning after your worst day retaining enthusiasm, then you have the major ingredient to help you succeed.
- Take time to recharge your batteries, which fuel your enthusiasm. Fatigue kills enthusiasm.

- CHAPTER 12 -
DRAINS – THE ENERGY SAPPERS

"Speak when you are angry and you will make the best speech you will ever regret".

Ambrose Bierce

Competitors become disappointed when expectations aren't met or if they have blown a winning position. This is the point at which they begin to perceive the contest as going against them. They begin to think regretfully about the blown opportunity and often roll out the excuses as to why they are in such a sad position.

When a player plays disappointingly it leads to self-pity or self-criticism, which results in a barrage of negative thoughts in the mind such as "Why did that net cord go against me?" or "How could I lose that game? I'm so bad". This process is damaging because it dampens any positive energy source that might be lingering. It is, however, highly common and for most of us incredibly hard to overcome. High-level accomplishments require mental toughness. Though apparently simple, mastering what you say or think in your mind requires tremendous discipline. All human beings slip up, especially under pressure, but the best competitors recover discipline over their thoughts quickly. Consequently they do not dwell on mistakes and therefore do not perpetuate them throughout the remainder of the contest.

In contrast, mentally weak competitors are easily distracted from the task, quickly losing discipline over what they think and say to themselves. It is incredible how often these competitors will openly tell their opponents verbally and with body language that they cannot control what they say or think about. They flip from anger to fear, from ranting and raving to moping about, and from competing intermittently to mentally fleeing the contest. In short, they become a complete jumble of conflicting energies and emotions. Not only does this have a detrimental effect on their performance, but it also feeds the confidence of their opponent.

Drains – The Energy Sappers

Quick points

- Mentally weak competitors are easily distracted.
- Mentally strong athletes compete with enthusiasm from the beginning to the end of a contest no matter what the score.
- Control the tone of voice in your head and what you say to yourself.

- CHAPTER 13 -
SELF-CONSCIOUSNESS AND BODY IMAGE

"Show me a guy who's afraid to look bad, and I'll show you a guy you can beat every time."

Lou Brock

Self-consciousness is an energy killer. It is the particular affliction of the teenager, but many adults suffer from it when put under the spotlight. There is no way of competing if your focus is on how you look or on what you perceive others to be thinking about you.

People freeze or become very stilted and nervous when they are self-conscious. It becomes difficult to co-ordinate limbs and the brain has difficulty thinking or remembering anything. We speak gibberish or stutter and become acutely paranoid that every error is being scrutinized. Beating the opponent is the last thing on our mind because the prime objective is to not make fools of ourselves.

Agassi famously revealed in his book that he was more focused on his hairpiece falling off than on winning the 1990 French Open final. This shows the amazing power that self-consciousness can have on a person, even an accomplished, world-class performer. In this energy state it is impossible to compete and win, so anyone who is unable to grow out of this feeling will not succeed in anything that requires focused performance.

This issue has to be dealt with and transformed into 'good nerves of anticipation' and enthusiastic energy. Often players are self-conscious because they are not confident in their ability. Practicing until they feel competent can overcome this problem.

The difficulty with self-consciousness is that the person feels that every move is being watched, and under that kind of scrutiny all faults will be seen. It is therefore hard to understand that people are generally thinking about themselves and are not very observant at all. I have had some success in combating self-consciousness by identifying what a player is self-conscious about and then asking the people around them if they had noticed this fact. Most often the answer has been 'no', which leads to a growing realization that they are merely magnifying the issue. Further ideas to lessen self-consciousness are:

- Ask the player to coach another player the skill that is the source of their embarrassment.
- Get the player to present or perform several times in front of a group until he is comfortable and confident in these situations.
- Identify times when he has performed well, nail down exactly what occurred in those situations and the thoughts that were in his mind, and work on reproducing this preparation that helped him remain uninhibited.

Female Athletes

Female athletes are under more pressure with regards to weight and body image. Weight is a delicate issue and needs to be approached with sensitivity, making reference to strength and muscular gains rather than a number on the scales. The scientific approach of skin folds or DEXA* scanning is more relevant and useful with female athletes. Additionally, it is appropriate to link gains in strength, power and endurance to their performance on court. There are direct correlations: improving squatting power equates to being able to hold low wide positions on court; improving jumping height helps explosion off the floor (serve and smash). These are two examples of linking physical gains to their tennis.

Creating an environment where the athlete is engaged in the process of measuring themselves against scientific targets is an excellent antidote to a negative focus on body image. It improves feelings of self-worth and promotes focus.

It is imperative for the female athlete to understand how nutrition can aid or damage their performance in their chosen sport. There are a lot of people claiming to be nutrition experts and keen to offer advice, but using a qualified sport nutritionist is imperative to ensure that nutrition can be tailored to the athlete's unique requirements and training plans. Learning about appropriate energy availability, portion control and timing of nutrients are fundamental for recovery, performance and body composition gains.

Female athletes who restrict their nutritional intake in order to manage their body fat composition without supervision, can do serious damage to their health. A restrictive diet will cause the stress hormone cortisol to increase and this has been linked to increased storage of fat. The athlete sees no improvement and then further decreases her intake, causing a negative impact on behaviour and consequently on performance.

Body image in athletes is rarely an issue when the programme takes care of education and strongly celebrates the physical gains that help the athlete perform their sport better. Sending the message that the athlete needs a body fit for purpose works well for dedicated athletes. Excellent female athletes will earn respect and embody a healthy look and lifestyle.

Quick points

- There is no way of competing if your focus is on how you look or on what you perceive others to be thinking about you.

- Often players are self-conscious because they are not confident in their ability, so practicing until they feel competent can overcome this problem.

- It is never as simple as calories in versus calories out. It is recommended that athletes and coaches seek personal education and professional nutritional advice.

*DEXA scan – dual energy x-ray absorptiometry measures bone density. Only necessary if there is concern by dietician/nutritionist that there are indicators such as a cessation of menstruation over many months.

- CHAPTER 14 -
FEAR AND NERVES

"Half of the failures in life come from pulling one's horse when he is leaping."
Thomas Hood

Fear is a source of negative energy and an energy sapper. Fear inhibits ability and drains a person of energy, leading to panicked and frozen performances. In other circumstances it will create nervous energy, which leads to rushing and often wanting the contest to end as swiftly as possible.

Nerves are unavoidable and must be converted into positive energy such as jumping about (e.g. Nadal) and positive self-talk with a 'getting up for a match feeling'. Nerves are good. They tell you that what you are about to do is important. They are there to help you get ready for the battle ahead. If you respond positively and transform the nervous energy into adrenaline, you will have energy to perform.

Conversely, if the nerves freeze your mind and body, you will be lethargic and fearful. You have to decide if you are going to let the nerves make you cringe, shrink, tremble, cower and shy away, or fight, compete and do battle. Even though it may not feel like it at the time, nerves give you a choice. Once you are aware of this you can begin to challenge yourself to use tools that enable you to approach a situation positively.

When engulfed by fear it is impossible to compete effectively. The mind is afraid, panicked, and unclear. The body cannot function smoothly or efficiently with so many conflicting and negative messages circulating through the nervous system. Fear often manifests itself through a player mentally fleeing the contest. They check-out and withdraw effort, waiting for the loss to arrive so they can leave the arena and the source of their fear and mental pain. Players in this state often remember almost nothing about the match after it is over.

The reasons why people are afraid are as numerous as the types of fear; fear of failure, of success, of parents or peers, organizations, coaches, or opponents. In my experience the fear of success is far greater than the fear of failure because it involves venturing into unknown territory – stepping out of the comfort zone. Competing at a level up from where you are is unnerving until you acclimatize and get used to your new status. It helps if you can actually identify and write down what your personal fears are. They have less power once you see them written down on paper. Anthony Robbins identifies fear as:

False

Evidence

Appearing

Real

A powerful tool I use in putting fear into context is to tell players that they are not afraid enough. I point out that if they think they are afraid, how would they react if a terrorist walked on court and told them they would be shot if they did not win? I venture that they would quickly realise what true fear was, improve focus, and perform well to save their lives. Similarly most players perform better when watched by a large crowd. The fear of not performing overcomes any other fear. Often when players are afraid they are in fact not putting enough pressure on themselves to perform and choose the easier route of just succumbing to the fear.

Another method I use is to challenge players with the question, "Do you truly wish to admit that other people in the same position are all better able to cope with the fear than you?"

I relay the story of how I was able to do a bungee jump simply by refusing to acknowledge that the teenagers ahead of me were mentally stronger and more capable of overcoming their fear than I was. And believe me I was terrified. When it came to my turn I told myself that if I had to jump to save myself from being shot I would not hesitate, so go!

It is important to understand that the key to managing your energy source is by controlling what you say to yourself. Players will often convince themselves that they are not good enough to win the match because they fear the strengths of their opponent. They become intimidated. When somebody tries to intimidate you it is usually because they are equally afraid. Use your imagination to develop techniques to keep your focus. One of the best ways to counterpunch being intimidated by someone is by picturing him or her naked on the loo. Humour can release a lot of stress.

Quick points

- A clear game plan helps keep stress and fear under control. Under pressure focus on your processes to deliver your plan.
- To succeed you will have to take risks and with risk comes some failure.
- Do you truly wish to admit that your opponents are all better at coping with the fear than you?
- Humour is often a good way to relax nerves.

- CHAPTER 15 -
MYTH OF THE INTROVERT

"Because I rant not, neither rave of what I feel, can you be so shallow as to dream that I feel nothing?"

R.D. Blackmore

I have come to the conclusion that there is no such thing as an introvert. I have worked with so many players who have started out shy and afraid of expressing themselves and seen them grow in confidence, stature and extraversion. It is my firm belief that introversion is situational.

As the success has grown for Federer, Nadal, Djokovic and Murray, their ability to express themselves in public has grown to the point where they are comfortable amongst Presidents, Prime Ministers and famous actors. Previously these situations would have stifled their ability to relax and be themselves. The most introverted athletes that I have encountered have situations where they are open and extroverted. This is generally at home with family or with close friends where they feel safe and secure. This is borne out time and again when players encounter their first tournaments, international junior tournaments, pro-tournaments and so on. They are incredibly uncomfortable and unable to ask established players to practice with them. They act like young kids at their first day in school. They fidget, avoid eye contact and generally try to stay out of the way and avoid making any obvious mistakes. Fast-forward to three or four tournaments down the line with a few wins under their belts and they are relaxed, joking, playing cards and part of the group.

I accept that there are degrees of introversion. However, I contend that familiarity in any situation lessens the fear, with the end result being that anyone can be very expressive once comfortable.

How does this help a tennis player? The power of awareness is immense. I explained this to a very introverted player and asked two questions.

1. Did he feel comfortable on a tennis court? He answered yes.

2. How could he explain being so uncomfortable in a match, having spent thousands of hours playing tennis and having just answered yes to question one? He could give no clear answer!

I explained the court was like his home and he was allowing opponents to dictate terms and make him uncomfortable in his own home. This was no different to someone staring into his lounge making him feel awkward. Instead, simply close the curtains, block them out, and get on with the job.

The solution was to understand that his discomfort was self-inflicted. He could no longer allow opponents to dictate how he acted and felt in his home, a place where he was normally so relaxed.

He improved substantially and his confidence grew in different environments. He realised that he needed to assess the situation and not just accept a default approach of being introverted. In any environment that he knew well and was normally comfortable, it was his duty to not be bullied into introversion through a lack of thought.

I urge all 'introverts' to look at their approach to situations and analyse if their discomfort is a default position. Anyone can choose differently and master their environment.

Quick points

- **It is my firm belief that introversion is situational.**
- **In time we can adapt and get comfortable in most situations.**
- **Do not fall into your default position without thought.**

- CHAPTER 16 -
ANGER

"My basic problem was that I would get all tripped out by the negatives – bad calls, bad days, and bad feelings – and anger got to be a habit. I was like a compulsive gambler or an alcoholic. Anger became a powerful habit."

John McEnroe

Anger is a powerful and immense source of energy, which is highly combustible and unsustainable over long periods. Using anger as an energy source is a dangerous strategy. Although it can achieve short-term success, it will always leave one feeling very flat and drained. It is also highly unreliable because it can adversely affect our thought processes. Many poor decisions are made during a fit of anger. Players who continually explode and draw on this energy to be aggressive rarely achieve success. The combination of poor decisions and flat periods ruin their ability to fight effectively and, as the losses pile up, the anger becomes increasingly negative and self-directed. Excuses and disappointment gain greater hold on the mind and the anger turns bitter, becomes more erratic, and adds to the confusion during the flat periods.

Competitors who learn to control anger can have better results. I call them "Simmerers". These people play with anger simmering under the surface. Although the energy levels are erratic because of the constant fight to keep control of the anger, they do have outbursts followed by periods of aggression that can turn matches in their favor. They have realised that exploding all the time is not the answer but when they attempt to remain calm they become flat, struggle for energy and discover that this state does not win matches.

Simmerers either have not worked out or have not been made aware of any energy source other than anger, so they continue to draw on this as their sole energy source. They try as best they can to keep a lid on it unless provoked to an exploding point. It is mentally tough for Simmerers to get through matches without exploding; a draining experience which ends either in the huge relief of winning or massive self-recrimination in losing. Matches become mini traumas and personal battles. Keep the lid on too tightly and

Anger

there is not enough energy; too loose and explosions occur. Even if the Simmerers are able to get the balance right, their focus on their personal battle is so strong that it is very tiring and difficult for them to ever see what their opponent is doing.

Unless you learn to draw on enthusiasm as the energy source, competing and winning consistently is impossible. 'What about the myriad of examples of successful angry people?' I hear you say. These can be easily explained. Anger can be very useful and highly effective to kick-start a listless performance. If it is short and sharp it can inspire bravery and aggression. However, it soon needs to be replaced by calm enthusiasm for the job at hand, which, at a high level, will always require calm decision-making and energy that is not draining.

Some people are able to use anger for controlled effect, recognize the loss of control quickly and transfer to using enthusiasm. Others use anger to become aggressive and overcome fear before transferring to another energy source. Although they can be highly unpleasant to watch or to work under, these people can also be very effective. However, they are always vulnerable because sometimes their loss of control gives their opponents the edge, which is often never relinquished.

If you analyse angry successful people, the time they spend in a contest being angry is actually minimal but the impact is often memorable. They have long periods of clear decision-making, unless the opponent is not good enough to challenge them, in which case they can afford to release anger without the risk of defeat.

> *"Clouded judgment has lost many a sportsman his victory."*
> McEnroe to Lendl in the French Open (1984)

McEnroe was the best player in the world at this time while Lendl had a reputation for choking* in Grand Slam finals (four up until that point). Lendl was being soundly beaten by McEnroe, two sets to love and was 2-4 in the third set when McEnroe went crazy at a line call on his serve, dropped serve and the set 7-5. He later said he got so angry because he felt he needed to finish the match quickly as he was feeling fatigued. The fact is that his anger confused his mind and he lost the match two hours later 7-5 in the 5th set. He would have been a lot less fatigued if he had remained focused and energised in the 3rd set.

It has to be said that Lendl himself never viewed the losses in the four finals as choking. He felt that he was still learning his trade and working out the final pieces of the jigsaw. It was his incredible mental strength and belief in the process that helped him to cope and continue with an optimistic attitude. He went on to win eight majors.

This fortitude and belief in process has enabled Lendl to help Andy Murray stem a small tendency to panic. Murray's focus on each step of the process led to greater confidence in the small improvements, which were enough to win the Olympics, The US Open and Wimbledon. The renewed alliance with Lendl in May 2016 has brought further success with Andy winning Wimbledon 2016 and a second Olympic gold medal.

It is clear that anger is a strong energy source but it is equally clear that it does more damage than good to the competitor, especially when sustained for any length of time. It is especially harmful when it emerges during the crunch time of a contest when clear thinking and handling pressure in a positive way are crucial to success.

Quick points

- **Anger is a powerful source of energy with a short life span.**
- **Anger often leads to poor decision-making, loss of focus and is ultimately the quickest way to lose.**
- **Anger can be very useful and highly effective to kick-start a listless performance.**
- **If you analyse angry successful people, the time they spend in a contest being angry is actually minimal, but the impact is often memorable. They have long periods of clear decision-making.**

- CHAPTER 17 -
LIBIDO

"Channel your energy - Focus."

Carl Lewis

Our libido, or sexual drive, is an incredibly powerful energy source and can be channeled into positive or negative action. It is, however, a positive energy and provides us with enormous drive to attain the attention of someone we find attractive.

The amount of fuel that people are capable of burning when chasing, flirting, planning a date, dancing, or staying up late when attempting to draw the attention of someone they are attracted to, is immense. This passion gives people the energy to act in powerful ways, which can be either productive or destructive. History is full of legacies of people who have driven themselves to great heights in order to win over, provide for, or impress a partner. Equally, they have been driven to break marriages, commit murder, or even start wars for love or pursuit of a partner.

The important distinction in whether this energy of attraction can lead to success or failure is where the focus lies in achieving the prize. A person can use enormous energy focusing on the game of pursuit, leaving less energy to use on his or her career. On the other hand they could use the bulk of the energy on their career, using spare time for pleasure and establishing relationships. There needs to be an understanding that there is work time, play time, and rest time.

If the balance is ample play time, ample work time, and little rest time, there are only an exceptional few who can succeed. These individuals have an excellent capacity to focus on purely one or the other of these activities. Most people, however, struggle to do this – their minds are either preoccupied with work, when they are trying to play, or vice versa. Some sportsmen achieve enough success during the party years to continue on to a great career. They often use their abilities as a tool in helping them create an edge over their rivals in the chase for partners.

The kudos associated with being a professional athlete motivates them to succeed and sometimes, if they have a genuine love for the sport, these individuals can begin to excel in their mid to late twenties when maturity gives them better balance. This is a precarious balance because often when they decide to focus more on their sport the window of opportunity has closed. Their story becomes the familiar "I could have been…"

Quick points

- **Libido is a powerful energy source that must be controlled.**
- **Libido must be channeled to provide more energy for the player's career.**

- CHAPTER 18 -
CREATING LOCKER ROOM POWER

"Do not let what you cannot do interfere with what you can do."

John Wooden

Locker Room Power is an aura built on attitude so it is crucial to adopt the right thoughts and feelings from the start. You need to create a picture in your mind of how you will look, play and behave after you have achieved your goals. This is a clear blueprint to work towards. A finished picture of the product that is you, the champion. You are effectively building an advertising campaign of your abilities as they develop. Remember this campaign is built on substance, not spin. The work, the preparation, the commitment, the improvement and the attitude must reflect the message your advertisement conveys to the outside world.

"The fight is won or lost far away from witnesses – in the mind, behind the lines, in the gym, and out there on the road, long before I dance under those lights."

The above quote from Ali shows how well he understood the work ethic necessary to create confidence and belief to win.

"I told the world I was the greatest. I figured if I told them often enough eventually they would believe me."

This second quote from Ali shows how astute he was at the age of 20. He knew that he was good, and if he could demonstrate a high quality in the ring the seeds of doubt would have already been planted into the mind of his opponent. Effectively opponents would begin to believe he was great.

Building LRP is about putting a number of things into place in your mind so you have a mental plan of where you are heading. This sets the physical work in motion.

To help you develop your personal aura, you will need to:

- Build your gameplan around the weapons that will hurt opponents.
- Build the powerful weapons first. These are the base of your confidence.
- Strengthen your weaknesses if they begin to undermine your ability to use your weapons effectively. Otherwise do not waste time trying to eliminate them.
- Build a vision of the end result and slowly work to merge the picture of where you are now into this future representation of yourself.

Many players hope to be successful but this hope is undermined by the bare fact that deep down they know they are not working hard enough. This causes them to hand over LRP to those players who are doing the work.

It is important to know what your current image is saying to the world at large. One of the best ways to do this is to watch a video recording of you walking onto court and playing a match. Is your demeanor showing someone confident and keen to play, or does it show someone negative, nervous and scared?

As well as managing your nerves, you will need to attend to and manage your locker room language. Never underestimate opponents or talk in a manner that can damage your reputation. Remember that locker room walls have eyes and ears! You never know who might be watching or listening, and the clubhouse lounges, gym, and restaurant are all an extension of the locker room.

Do not be afraid to put out positive publicity if it is true. For example, if you have just finished a tough physical block and are fitter than ever before, it is okay to tell people. This message only becomes powerful, however, if your actions support what you say. For instance, show in practice a desire to chase every ball. Your extra speed and endurance also need to be evident in your matches. Your LRP is cemented when an opponent thinks 'Wow, this guy wasn't kidding when he said he was fit'. Furthermore, he will tell other players after the match, regardless of whether he won or lost.

Creating Locker Room Power

"LRP starts with substance. It then encompasses the perception as well as the substance. It occurs when people begin to exaggerate the depth of your weaponry and opponents begin to feel that they need to play above themselves to compete with you. On any level this is double-edged. Opponents think you are invincible and in turn you begin to feel immensely confident.
This combination is very hard to beat."

David Sammel

Anyone can create Locker Room Power. If they train smart and choose their language carefully they will become their own advert reflecting their great attitude towards competition.

If you advertise a bad product well, it can work against easily impressed and inexperienced players. But bluffing is not sustainable in the long run. The key is to make sure the product is good; the advertising will then simply reinforce the product, adding to the perceived truth and potency of the LRP.

Coaches and trainers attempt to find ways for players to believe in themselves, but they ignore LRP at their peril. It is important to understand this factor, because most matches and tournaments are still won by snowballing momentum.

A player's LRP can build during a tournament when he wins a match and begins to ride a wave of confidence. This temporary force can become the start of lasting LRP. The real deal, however, is someone who backs up a good performance with consistent excellence. Use the momentum of a tournament victory or an exceptional result to work harder and galvanize your attitude. In other words, if you bask in the comfort of one big result it can fade into the 'flash in the pan' category.

Andy Murray is an example of a player whose temporary LRP nearly gave him the breakthrough he needed to cement a real feeling of fear in his opponents at the very top level. He went into the Australian Open 2009 having generated LRP by defeating the two best players in the world, Nadal and Federer, in tournaments leading up to the event. Seemingly the alpha male, he lost narrowly to Verdasco in the quarter-finals, which revealed the status of his LRP to be temporary at the highest level. Had he won the tournament, his LRP would have rocketed and become established at the top of the tour. He eventually managed to cement his LRP with two Olympic golds, two Wimbledon titles and the US Open.

Quick points

- LRP is built on substance, not spin.
- It is important to know what your current image is saying to the world at large.
- Any person can create Locker Room Power by training smart, choosing the language used carefully, and producing an advertisement that reflects a great attitude towards competition.
- Use the momentum of a tournament victory or an exceptional result to work harder and galvanize your attitude.

- CHAPTER 19 -
CONSOLIDATING LOCKER ROOM POWER

"You have to defeat a great player's aura more than his game."

Pat Riley

Over the years many of the world's top athletes have commented on how difficult it is to remain successful once they have achieved success. The consolidation of success is an arduous task. It is a task that requires a different set of skills from those required to become successful.

"Locker Room Power is the perception that a player is better than he actually is, generated by other players talking about his game in a way that creates a positive aura."

Sustaining LRP at any given level is achieved when you compete for every match with the discipline that got you there. You need to keep your work ethic and use your new-found confidence to continually set higher standards for yourself. At the very top, no one will bring you a chair for the table. You must bring one yourself.

There will almost certainly come a time when you lose a few matches in a row. This will test your discipline. All eyes will be watching to see if you can manage a bad spell without letting it develop into a crisis of confidence. Respect from other players means that a few bad results will be perceived as a glitch rather than a crisis.

The secret of sustained Locker Room Power and success is learning how to become comfortable with being uncomfortable.

If you keep your discipline, the moment you win again you will be accepted as the real deal and someone who belongs at that level. It is at this precise moment – when you feel comfortable at this new level and you are accepted – that you should make yourself uncomfortable again by raising your standards. It is this intent that will keep you at the level you are at, or help you move higher. Raising standards is the finest guard against complacency and loss of Locker Room Power, which can quickly drop you down a level or two.

Most players, and certainly all champions, are continually trying to improve. If your aim is solely to stay where you are you will quickly find yourself falling behind. Remember, consolidating locker room power is not a relaxing time. It is the time when you must show the most fight and the most discipline.

Quick points

- **Locker Room Power is fostered by the environment you and your team create.**

- **All eyes will be watching to see if you can manage a bad spell without letting it develop into a crisis of confidence.**

- **You need to maintain your work ethic and use your new-found confidence to set higher standards for yourself.**

- **At the very top no one will bring you a chair for the table. You must bring one yourself.**

- CHAPTER 20 -
LOCKER ROOM POWER CASE STUDY

"Your attitude, not your aptitude, will determine your altitude."

Zig Ziglar

My experience leads me to believe that whatever your circumstances, if you adopt the right attitude, LRP can work for you. The following case study is about Martin Lee, a superb tennis player I worked with previously. The story describes how he acquired locker room power during his career and, as you will discover, handed it away.

Case Study

In December 2000 I began working with Martin Lee (Marty), a former world number one junior player and one of the brightest talents in British tennis. He was not progressing as quickly as both he and others expected when he sought my help. We began with me observing a couple of his matches, and working hard in between on general drills to sharpen his game. It was not until after this initial evaluation period that we were able to discuss what I believed were the specific areas for him to address in order for him to achieve his ambition of being a top 100 player.

I identified the following three areas of priority – the weapons that would build confidence and deliver the necessary fear factor:

1. The inside out (off) forehand.

Although this was already a weapon, it was unreliable as it was being hit too flat. Better footwork and consistently hitting the shot with more spin would result in a greater net clearance and more jump off the court. Any loss in speed (from hitting a flat shot) would be more than compensated for by increased width and most importantly a very high consistency.

2. The return of a second serve.

Quick footwork and the ability to hit a backhand (as well as a forehand) return on the rise would open up a great opportunity to attack second serves and follow them into the net.

3. Net play.

Better volleys would enable Marty to back up his ability to attack second serves. This would put increased pressure on his opponents, forcing them to go for smaller targets when passing.

Because we knew clearly how we would improve his game, designing interesting practice was easy. After seven months of hard work on these priority areas, Marty's improvements were evident. The Tour began to realise that he was a player on a mission – his ranking was rising and opponents feared his style of play. In 2001, after achieving success in Challengers (see glossary) and with a good display in the French Open, qualifying, behind him, he found himself on the Centre Court at Wimbledon against Tim Henman in the 2nd round. Although his game was ready for this challenge, mentally he was not quite prepared for such a big stage. Although he turned in a reasonable performance, he was too respectful of his opponent and played too passively, his level of aggression not high enough to truly challenge. The week after Wimbledon he continued to build on his achievements and reached the final of Newport, a Tour event. This raised his ranking to 103 in the world, nearly reaching the goal set for the end of the year and earning him direct acceptance into the US Open.

The build-up to the US Open was brilliant. Jez Green (physical trainer) accompanied us as we set about a punishing yet practical mental, physical and tennis-training regime focused on a powerful showing at the Open. The mentality we developed during the lead up was gained through linking the physical pain of intense training to his mind. If he could take this training on and off the court and link it to being tough in matches then he would be a contender in New York. The message was 'Why go through all this if you are not going to show the same mental and physical endurance in matches?' I also spoke to him consistently about not being afraid to use this mentality against anyone. This mentality needed to become a way of life.

Case Study

Marty qualified for Montreal, losing narrowly to Bohdan Ulirach (World No 30 at the time) and beat James Blake in Long Island. By the time he took to the court in New York against Dutch player Sjeng Schalken (World Number 22 at the time) he was ready.

Few people gave Marty a chance against Schalken. However, as a team we believed otherwise and most importantly so did Marty. Over the previous 10 months, through his work ethic and committed game style, he had built a growing reputation that he was becoming a genuine Tour player.

The match was an example of enhancing a reputation (through LRP) even though Marty lost. Only a flash of brilliance enabled Sjeng to convert his only break point of the 5th set. After a 4 ½ hour battle, Marty had proved he could consistently compete with one of the best players in the world. This was endorsed by a post-match conversation between the two players as they warmed-down on the bikes in the gym. Sjeng said: "That was a battle. Keep going and you will be top 50 in no time." The important message here for Marty was, when established players recognize and accept that a player is coming through, the next step for the player on the rise is to continue focusing on his work ethic. This sends out the message that he is not only giving notice of his arrival, but also that his intention is to continue to get better both physically and mentally.

Marty did develop and enhance enough LRP to achieve his goal, reaching 94 in the world early in 2002. But he did not consolidate his LRP as well as he might have done. Marty had a definite goal of top 100 and once this was achieved it was my opinion that this affected his focus and commitment. It was this belief which caused me to end our time together after a poor performance in the 2002 Australian Open where he caved in against Francisco Clavet of Spain, losing 7-6 6-1 6-0. Jez and I felt he had let himself down with excuses and I said he should call me when he was ready to commit to the next goal of top 50.

You should never become complacent just because you have reached a goal. Assess the options going forward and re-set. Satisfied players slip backwards. With your coach and support team continue to move forwards with as much determination as previously. Once you have momentum, let it to take you forwards to the next phase of your journey.

Quick points

- Create an identity for yourself or the team.
- If you know clearly what you need to improve, designing interesting practice is easy.
- Create a culture that aids the growth of your identity.
- Adopt the right attitude – you will need desire, self-belief and commitment.
- Satisfied players slip backwards.

- CHAPTER 21 -
COMPLACENCY AND ARROGANCE

"For one to expect or ask things of others that he himself, if asked, would not be willing to do or give, is the worst kind of arrogance."

Anthony Beal

Complacency is a fairly common occurrence. Players get complacent when they fall for a false belief that 'once I reach my goal I will be able to relax and reap the rewards of my hard work'.

When players reach a goal they usually attain it on a wave of momentum and confidence. If they take their foot off the gas, nothing goes wrong for a considerable period of time because of the confidence and the excitement that accompanies this breakthrough. This positive energy will compensate for any shortcuts being taken. However, when the inevitable losses begin to occur, the work ethic, which is the real backbone of confidence, is not in place and the player can easily fall through the floor. LRP is lost because the other players know instinctively that the newfound status was only temporary.

A good opponent will be quick to notice a player's complacency and use it to his advantage, realizing that it gives him a chance to attack and change the momentum in the match. True competitors do not respect complacency.

Arrogance

Arrogance based on confidence, self-belief and a valid work ethic can be a strength, even though it is sometimes ugly to watch. However, when it is based on a lack of respect for opponents, to the point where it is no longer possible to perceive the danger an opponent may possess or the improvements they have made, it becomes a weakness.

Arrogance can have another consequence that is equally damaging – when a player no longer thinks that he can learn from anyone because he knows best. Arrogance can lead to complacency, such as the presence of the 'I'm so good I don't need to work as hard' attitude. Over-confidence in tennis spells doom, because over-confident people do not take care of details.

Like complacency, arrogance is not an attitude that most good players respect. In fact, it can be a player's downfall. A competitive opponent will often get fired up by arrogance on the other side of the net and be determined not to let the opponent's head get any bigger by doing everything possible to ensure an arrogant player does not come off the court with a win.

Perhaps one of the best examples of youthful arrogance was the drama played out during the 1999 French Open final between Martina Hingis and Steffi Graf. Having won the singles and doubles at the Australian Open at the beginning of the year, Hingis was having a stellar year. She found herself in the final of the French Open facing veteran Steffi Graf, who had not won a grand slam event in three years. Graf considered herself a surprise finalist, admitting frankly that she had entered the French Open that year just to help her fine-tune her tournament skills and sharpen her game for Wimbledon. Graf, almost 30 years of age, faced the dynamic, smiling 18 year-old from Switzerland in one of the most memorable contests in the history of French Open finals.

Hingis played great tennis, taking the first set 6-4 and leading 2-0 in the second set. Then the bottom fell out of her well-ordered, self-assured world. She disputed a line call. Her ball was called out, she felt the ball had hit the line. Hingis asked the umpire to check the line, which she did. The call stood. Hingis then walked over to Graf's side of the net and pointed to the mark she felt proved her point. This was arrogance in full bloom. It was also grounds for a penalty point. You cannot cross over to the opponent's side of the net in tennis. Hingis knew that and did it anyway. Still the umpire did not penalize her.

Hingis refused to play on and instead asked for the tournament referee. This was her key error. The referee came on court, denied Hingis an overrule and imposed a penalty point. Hingis lost the argument, her composure and her momentum. The French crowd, already pulling for Graf, became absolutely hostile toward Hingis. Graf won the game and the score stood at 2-1. The wrangling continued into the next game when a call went against Graf. Hingis held and went 3-1 up but Graf, spurred on by the support, broke back and went on to win the set. The crowd continued to chant 'Steffi', cheered Hingis's errors and booed her when she took a toilet break at one set all.

Hingis was never a factor in the 3rd set. The crowd booed her when in desperation she served underarm to save a match point, a tactic that was applauded when Michael Chang (who had severe cramp) used it against Ivan Lendl in the 1989 Men's semi-final. Hingis lost the set 6-2. Graf won the match as much as Hingis lost it, but both were heavily impacted by the French crowd. As Graf grew in strength from the support, Hingis's capacity was diminished by the acrimony. Her self-assured arrogance and anger cost her dearly in this match (she was only 18) and the crowd was unforgiving. It was not a fair fight. She left the court in tears; breaking down completely once the match was over. This match was an opportunity for her to add a French Open title to her career, but it was never to be. Her arrogance clouded her judgment and perspective of how far ahead she was in the match, causing her to disrespect a great champion and tournament. Ultimately, this denied her a chance to win a grand slam on all surfaces.

Quick points

- Complacency often arises when a goal is reached and the perception is that life ought to be easier.
- It is important to continue the work ethic that helped achieve the goal.
- Arrogance can cloud judgment.
- Arrogance can lead to complacency and impair learning if the person believes that they know all.

- CHAPTER 22 -
GOALS FROM THE HEART

"Your goal should be to build your reputation as someone who calmly works to get better."

David Sammel

When I first began coaching it seemed sensible and professional to evaluate a pupil's entire game and then set goals to improve each area. This impressed players and parents, but I soon realised that all these objectives overwhelmed players and actually hurt confidence with thoughts of how much was wrong with their games and how much work was to be done. Nowadays I still fully evaluate their whole game and then rank the work needed to improve in order of priority, but I do so privately. I present to the players only two objectives. Once we have made significant gains I introduce two further areas of work that need improving. In the background I can achieve gains in other areas without drawing attention to them.

When discussing career goals we paint the inspirational dream and then forget about it, concentrating on setting game improvement objectives over a three month period and an annual ranking target. The evaluation dates are simply that. I'm adamant that players do not evaluate a three month achievement goal before the end, because often the best comes in the last week or so. Constant evaluation creates nervousness and frustration if things do not go well early on. Outcome goals, like an end of year ranking target, are a good idea. (We cannot pretend that they do not exist and rankings can fuel ambition.) I always stress that these goals are the icing on the cake. The process goals of how players will improve are the nuts and bolts of a career. It is pointless and harmful to plan to succeed by a certain date, because tennis will almost certainly test your resolve by missing many an outcome deadline.

Amazing achievements can happen when players settle into a process. Desire, with a smart work ethic and self-belief, means there is no ceiling on personal achievements until the journey is done. This may mean winning an Olympic gold, running a marathon in 3½ hours, or losing 20lbs in weight. It is the combination of your intent and actions, which, if congruent with your target, will unleash a powerful force and energy that will help you accomplish your goal. If your actions are matched with pure desire and commitment, the world takes notice of this intensity and focus.

Apart from process goals the coach must educate the player to understand the importance of honesty and the necessity for consistently good habits. These two objectives are sometimes overlooked in goal setting. Good routines in preparation allow players to deal with issues before they step out to perform and help them acquire the consistency that every competitor craves. The aim is to limit surprises to external events.

Honesty is needed from the player to take the responsibility of dealing with or highlighting any internal issues before stepping out on court. Young competitors, and even many experienced players, tend to brush concerns under the carpet rather than dealing with them and finding solutions. I encourage players to develop a plan to handle the problem before walking on court.

> *"What you get by achieving your goals is not as important as what you become by achieving your goals."*
>
> Zig Ziglar

We all evolve during our lives, but rarely will we develop more than during the transition from teenager to adult. What will never change is that we will always perform better and do better when we are doing things that we enjoy. Encouraging teenagers therefore, to follow their passion will facilitate happier and more motivated people. Naturally there are boundaries such as working within the confines of the law and creating awareness that even pleasurable pursuits require work and dedication in order to excel. Allowing them to think short-term, and by that, I mean follow their current heart, with the proviso that they do it with all their might and focus, will help them confirm or eliminate careers through personal experience rather than through the prism of others.

> *"Who knows where it will lead, but one thing is certain - doing what you enjoy as well as you can, gives you self-respect and mini wins every day"*
>
> David Sammel

Goal setting has traditionally been based on a logical progression that has always bothered me because everyone is different. A rational goal, set to a realistic time span sounds great and is usually the obvious next step, but a goal from the heart is not always the logical next step. Sometimes the goal can be as small as consolidating a current gain. It can be very helpful to consider that time is a measurement and useful for inspiration, not the goal. If a target is not reached in a set time this is not an indicator of failure, but rather a miscalculation of the time needed to reach the goal.

Time is a 'motivator', not the objective.

It is equally important to separate shorter-term goals from a dream or vision. Having a clear picture of your dream is important because that will provide the motivation for doing the labour of love (work) to get there, but a dream or vision must be seen as a destination that will require many goals along the way. The dream is usually so far ahead in the future that it is best to choose it and then forget about it and focus on each step needed until you are close enough to the summit that you can see it as a reality. Constant focus on the summit at the start can lead to daydreaming and belief that it is easier to achieve or not too far away which in turn can encourage delusion.

> *"The first principle is that you must not fool yourself, and you are the easiest person to fool."*
> Richard Feynman (Nobel prize-winning physicist)

Another factor is that each goal will require full concentration and allowing the mind wander too far into the future will affect the quality of the work needed to take place in the present to achieve each small step forward. Although this is another huge subject on its own, it is helpful if early on there is perspective and acknowledgement that achieving a dream is not a final destination. Once realised, life will go on and new targets will need to be set, or the deflation of finally achieving a dream will be significant, especially if it has been a long-term life ambition.

> *"Dreaming about being an actress is more exciting than being one."*
> Marilyn Monroe

Set goals from your heart, goals you know in your mind that you can and will achieve, rather than those, which are expected or sound good. This is why New Year resolutions often fail. Pledging that you will go to the gym five times a week, knowing full well, for you, that this is an unrealistic promise and a mountain to climb, and that you will almost certainly let yourself down, ultimately makes you feel a failure. Failure cultivates an excuse mentality, which leads to frivolous wishes. When your own words cannot to be taken seriously, you will have little trust in yourself and therefore little confidence. Athletes who make excuses often over time learn that these justifications and feeling sorry for themselves are the real reasons for slow improvement.

Honesty is vital in facing difficulties and in finding solutions to overcome problems. Set a goal that you can and will achieve such as "I will do planks at home three times a week and aerobic exercise for twenty minutes once a week." When this goal is achieved for a sustained period you will feel good about yourself and build trust in your goal setting. This trust will lead to increased motivation and a desire to add extra to your programme.

Goals from the heart succeed because they build belief and pride in your own word and give you confidence to do more, motivated by the constant success. In sport, good coaches know that there is no magic bullet and small gains with good habits over time underpin outstanding achievement. (Read the "Play to Gain" chapter in the book Locker Room Power.)

I discourage long-term goals set in stone, for the world is ever-changing. An ambition such as becoming an architect is fantastic but keep your mind open to the fantastic adventure of life. An architect might design a house for a TV producer, who asks for advice on the design for a movie set. Through this project, a realisation that her skills can be used in set design, which she thoroughly enjoys, suddenly leads to the idea of changing career. Although it means less money, less certainty, she takes the plunge and a couple of years down the line she receives an invite to work at Disney and moves to California where she meets her future husband... A healthy focus on short-term goals from the heart that gives you a wow factor, makes even the hardest challenges fun. If the focus is too future based and wrapped up in achieving a goal no matter what, even when your heart is telling you that it is no longer what you want, then your mind will be blinded to any new and wonderful opportunities and a fear of change. What we want out of life is very personal and can evolve. This is not failure.

> *"It is good to have an end to journey toward;*
> *but it is the journey that matters, in the end."*
>
> Ernest Hemingway

There are rare individuals who know from a young age what they want and have a burning passion for the career that never changes, but others are serial go-getters in many fields with varied interests and talents.

> *"Changing a goal constantly when the work gets difficult is a recipe for disaster and we all know the difference, which is why we need to consider carefully what dream fires our passion and allows us to truly set goals from our heart."*
>
> David Sammel

Quick points

- Prioritize process and improvement goals ahead of outcome targets such as ranking.
- Delay evaluating goals until the end of the period as the progress might come in the final weeks.
- Time is a measurement not a goal.
- Set goals from the heart. Constant success builds trust and confidence in your ability, not only in setting achievable goals, but also in your dependability to follow through and succeed.
- It is okay to evolve and change direction.
- Know the difference between quitting because the work has gotten tough and a genuine desire to change direction.
- Honesty in what you genuinely want and will do to achieve a goal is vital to succeeding

- CHAPTER 23 -
INJURY

Dealing with injury is difficult. Injury forces athletes to re-evaluate goals and their journey. It can often be an extremely valuable time, a chance to gain perspective and look closely at their goals and how to achieve them.

It is important for the injured player and the coach to work with all parties involved in the recovery and rehab such as the surgeon, physiotherapist and physical trainer to lay out a plan for a clear road back which includes realistic time scales.

The coach has to emphasise the benefits of making gains in other areas until the player sees the injury as an opportunity to improve parts of his body or mind through detailed work that in normal training would never get this type of attention. Although injury is frustrating it is also an opportunity to refresh the player's appreciation of how important the sport is to them and energise their mind with new goals.

Quick points

- Injury can be an opportunity for a player to make gains in areas that fail to get attention during normal training.
- Injury is an opportunity to evaluate goals and perspective.
- Time out can refresh an athletes mind.

- CHAPTER 24 -
COURAGE

"Courage is going from failure to failure without losing enthusiasm."

Sir Winston Churchill

One of the most important virtues for a person to have is courage. Within sport those players who we, the spectators, classify as courageous, are usually near the peak of their sport. But do we actually know what courage is in sport? Is it the ability to hit a blinding winner down the line on match point down? Is Serena Williams courageous for returning to world number 1 after her life-threatening illness? And is there such a thing as collective courage? Are the women that campaigned for equal rights between male and female athletes courageous?

The following is an interview with Samantha Murray a top British tennis player with Louise Scott, a sport psychologist and colleague. Louise investigates Sam's story in which they discuss courage.

Louise sets the stage. Sam was a good junior who decided to take up a scholarship to Northwestern University near Chicago where she played for four years and graduated with a degree in Economics. She came to *TeamBath in September 2010 and told David she was ready to play pro tennis. In 2011 she was the third fastest climber in the world going from unranked to 380 in the world. She has subsequently reached a career high of 165, becoming British number four. What was remarkable was her courage to totally remodel her slice forehand into a topspin forehand, a difficult change as an adult. A leading coach told David that she had no chance of success with that forehand. David replied sharply "That is true – but she won't have that forehand". The work put in to developing a topspin forehand, that is now a weapon, and the trust that Sam gave to David is an example of a powerful relationship between a player and coach.

Louise (LS): "Sam, thank you very much for participating in this interview. If you could start by describing what you think courage is in tennis?"

Sam (SM): "I think courage is... I think it's being able to do what you want to do, like sticking to your own game, and not being dictated to by your opponent, just sort of having faith that what you're doing is the right thing, even if things aren't going so well."

LS: "How then, would you describe a courageous person? What sort of characteristics would they have?"

SM: "I think part of it is not worrying about what other people think of you, and that would be your results or game style or the type of person you are, you know, sticking to what feels good for you. I would say not being influenced is a big thing, being truthful to yourself, and also I think these types of people are not scared of failing. They keep trying until it works out."

LS: "So courageous players acknowledge what their game is and who they are, and they then persevere with that? Even if results and performances aren't going as planned it's just a case of trusting, and saying to yourself this is me, this is the way I'm going to play?"

SM: "Yes. Personally my game is quite high-risk, and I find it more fun playing that way but I do go through stages where it's not working. At the beginning of my pro career it was easy to fall back and try and make balls, and that goes well to a certain point and level, but if you want to get higher than that then you have to stick with your instinct. My instinct, or the way I want to play tennis, is high-risk and for me that takes courage to acknowledge and stick with your game and to not be influenced by others. I think my game style requires a certain degree of courage... you know, winning the points instead of wanting my opponent to give them to me is really important. Being forthright enough to be the player that is aggressive and who wins points from winners and forcing opponents into errors is a big thing."

LS: "Great. Was there a point in your career where you thought maybe 'I am a courageous player' or was there an experience that challenged your courage? I mean you said before about not letting an opponent or external influence change your game; was there a landmark moment where you made the decision to play your game and purely your game?"

SM: "Yeah definitely, I have had a couple of those. Dave has always been saying "your game is to hit the ball so make sure you hit it." And maybe it was two years ago when I was playing this one match, a girl who was a lot higher ranked than me, and I consciously told myself I was going to hit the ball the whole way through, and when I came off the court I said to Dave that I felt completely out of control for the whole match. He said to me that it was the best match I had ever played. And it was so weird, because it felt like I was going to have a heart attack the whole way through the match and it felt almost like I wasn't trying. He said no, that it was the complete opposite because it was the first time I had just played my game the whole way through, like 100% percent. I'm not exaggerating with the heart attack thing, it was just a completely alien feeling where you go for everything when it's there to go for no matter what the consequences. That was the first time I did it and then the second time was last May 2012 in Japan when I'd been having a bit of a rough time, not playing great and I was feeling like I was pushing the ball. Dave laid it on the line and said if I did not hit the ball I would have no career. Before the next match I was determined that I was going to hit the ball no matter what, from the first ball to the last, and even though I lost quite easy (I think it was 3 and 3), I had some chances. But from then on, I have not gone back. I mean there have been short periods here and there but never a whole match. As an overall thing I have changed, prepared to play my game and my game only. Those were the main moments, and it felt like if I go back then I won't ever improve or get better; so I guess for me that was a courageous decision to make, even though I hadn't thought about it like that before."

LS: "And do you think Dave has had an impact on that as well?"

SM: "Yes absolutely. Dave just, cut it out basically. He was like "First of all you can stop that. I don't care that you won; you didn't play your game. Where you want to get to, playing like that simply won't cut it." That was a big thing that forced me to think long term. I could hack away and win matches at 600 in the world but if I actually wanted to get much higher, which I did, then I had to stick to the way I wanted and needed to play. I understand that its tougher and higher risk but you know, nobody said it was easy."

LS: "It is definitely a hugely personal battle then, where you have to 100% be prepared to take the risk…"

SM: "Well personally, to start with it's more fun and enjoyable to me to play that way, as much as losing is horrible. I know ultimately it's the only way I am going to win… I mean I know it will take time, but now I know when I start to push the ball, and I hate it when I do as it feels awful, so it's taken a bit of time but I fully understand that going forward is the only way. And Dave's overall message is that don't worry, tennis starts at 300, and below that it's irrelevant apart from what you learn."

LS: "Just going back to the heart attack feeling. Could you describe how that felt?"

SM: "It felt quite scary to be honest and it was very uncomfortable. I felt out of control. That's the best word I can use… you know just swinging freely… and I definitely lost the consciousness of effort because as I say it felt like I wasn't trying but I obviously was…it was scary though. I don't know if it was adrenaline or whatever, because my mind was calm, but afterwards my whole body was shaking…"

LS: "And that was your best performance?"

SM: "Up to that point yes… Even though I lost it was the closest I had come to beating a girl of that standard."

LS: "And that performance gave you confidence even though you lost it?"

SM: "Yes afterwards… after I'd thought about it… because it's the closest I'd got to a player of that level. Looking back it was a big turning point. My family was watching and they hadn't seen me in a while and they said exactly the same thing that it was the best I had ever played."

LS: "If you played a match like that now would you analyse it differently?"

SM: "God yes, it is normal for me… like I have probably played a ton of those matches since, because I'm playing people who are that level and better now and I've not had the same feeling… so just sitting here now thinking about it, it's quite pleasing to see how far I've come in that respect… I've never actually thought about it properly."

LS: "So the age old question then, is it more about the performance than the outcome for you or a mixture of the two?"

SM: "I think to some extent it is – not the performance with regards to me executing everything perfectly – but more to do with the intent behind the performance I think, because we all have days where we hit the ball like we haven't played tennis before and that's tough to control, but what you absolutely can control is the intent behind the performance."

LS: "So would you say that there is a link between intent and courage?"

SM: "Yeah for sure, I think the intent takes courage. But it's hard to keep that intent, and you know maybe when you want to back off and you are tired, then it takes a lot to stick to the original intent."

LS: "Has there been a match of yours where you displayed this intent when playing poorly?"

SM: "Yeah, I think I played a match in Australia that had a number of courageous moments. I hadn't been winning many matches and lost a couple of tough 3-setters to good players. I was quite heavily down like 4-1 in a set and I started to play a lot better and brought it back and got to a 3rd set tie break and I pretty much went mad and served and volleyed for most of the time. She clearly didn't like it, and it was obviously very high-risk, but it was the way to beat her and if I executed it then I won and if I didn't then at least I had the comfort of trying to use my game. And it worked. I won that one and from there on the rest of the trip went a lot better and one win and one moment turned it around. Having that intent was hugely influential. For me I think that is courage… throwing in those kinds of points in big moments, and if anything I think it threw her a bit, like shocked her."

LS: "Going back to what you were saying about Dave do you think that courage can be instilled by creating the right environment or do you think you're either born with it or you aren't?"

SM: "I think part of it is personality and some people clearly struggle to take risks, and taking risks doesn't motivate them, but for me, apart from tennis I wouldn't say that I am a really high-risk person. I'm not a worrier but I'm not an adrenaline junkie either, but my game is high-risk and I think I have developed the courage to keep playing that in tough situations, and if Dave hadn't kept telling me to do it, I don't personally think I would have done it. I think the environment you're in has a massive impact on you, whether you are a courageous tennis player or not."

Courage

LS: "Very interesting, shows how important culture and the players' environment is. So now you're at Bath, can you see other players around you working on, or going down a similar path to you?"

SM: "I can pick out people who are working on it for sure… and I can spot the ones who definitely aren't courageous, you know… a mile off sometimes. And to be fair to them, some have come from elsewhere and have only just begun working with Dave, and they have started to show signs of playing their own games more regularly, persevering more often…but it's a battle."

LS: "So you believe and accept that in order to become successful you would need to possess some elements of courage?"

SM: "Yeah definitely. Without doubt. And when I play my best when I take more chances, or I take the chances and make them… but what I need to work on is even when I'm not playing well to take the chance anyway, and I am getting better at that, I know it's something that I need to do."

LS: "What has been stopping you from doing that?"

SM: "I'm not sure whether its doubt or inexperience of doing it on the big points on the big stages… I don't think I've played enough… I mean it took me about 6 months to start to shift from the college mentality to pro mentality. It took me a while to understand whether I was pushing or hitting the ball, but the tournaments in Japan and Australia for me were definite markers of my changing mentality, where I made the decision to go and hit the ball and play my game… I mean thinking about it now there have been matches since where I have played big points and I haven't gone for it, but those are few and far between now and overall my intent is 100% to play my game."

LS: "Does your previous performance or result impact on your intent?"

SM: "Yeah to a degree, like I played a good tournament in Glasgow and played four matches really well, so I had good confidence and momentum… but in the 2nd set of the final I backed off a little and during the 3rd set changeover I remember consciously saying to myself to go after it and take it from her and the confidence and momentum helped me to carry out that intent. Another part is just thinking clearly. When confidence is high you just do things, there isn't a lot of conscious thought, but when things become a bit shaky you do start to think more, which hinders performance."

LS: "Ok, so are you prepared to be more courageous and have more intent against someone who is higher ranked than you or somebody who is lower ranked than you?"

SM: "High ranked for sure, because part of it is that you have to be courageous against the better players or they will just punish you... I mean sometimes it's not the ranking you know... you soon realise that if you just put the ball in against someone then it will be smacked back... but I think the higher ranking does give you some sort of freedom as well... like you have a freedom to show what you can do and if it works then great and if it doesn't then you're not expected to win so that makes it a bit easier... like in Japan I had one of my best results against a girl who was well in the top 100 and the way I beat her was coming forwards and executing things well... not the whole way through because it was really long 3-setter, but on the key points I executed well and I won 8-6 in the final set tiebreak. Then the next day I played a Thai girl who was a similar level to me and I knew that she couldn't hurt me if I played my game... but I got nervous and thought about too many things and stopped playing aggressively, and I think that's the pressure thing... because if I took chances against the first girl and missed them then so be it, but against this girl even though she still was higher ranked than me I knew that my game was better than hers and I thought I should never lose to her... and that thought was the killer. I got through but it was unnecessarily ugly."

LS: "Is it harder to be courageous when you perceive yourself to be in control of the match or out of control?"

SM: "In control for sure, because I think it's easier to go for stuff when they are pressuring you. When you're in control, it is tempting to wait for them to give it to you. This is when I have to remind myself to keep high energy and point by point take the match away from them."

LS: "That's great Sam thank you, really interesting stuff."

Louise summarises. The interview reveals insightful information regarding Sam's opinions on courage in tennis. Throughout the interview Sam focused very much on acknowledging what her game was. She then spoke in great detail about the challenges and hardships she has gone through to allow herself to play her game without being influenced by others. There is very much a sense of finding your own identity as a tennis player and sticking with it regardless of the circumstances. This involves a large amount of self-examination, which takes courage.

It is essential but difficult for athletes to take a long hard look at themselves because they will not always like what they find. Additionally, Sam noted that to be successful, a degree of courage needs to be part of their make-up. We then went on to discuss how players develop courage. Is it part of their personality or can it be taught? Sam spoke about the environments she was in and how they shaped her. She described how the college environment didn't foster the development of courage within a player, nor did it foster individuality. However, the environment that Dave has put together at Bath allowed Sam and others to acquire characteristics of courage.

This is an important point, because training centers can have a huge impact on their players. An environment that aids the growth of players with encouragement and patience to allow changes to occur, then players develop without fear. I know that Dave has worked and continues to work very hard on creating a winning culture through adventure and bravery at the Academy.

Quick points

- **Courage is the intent to play your game whether you are playing well or not.**
- **Courage in tennis is going for everything when it's there to go for, no matter the consequences.**
- **Environment either fosters courage or diminishes it.**

- CHAPTER 25 -
CONSISTENT HABITS FOR EFFECTIVE MIND MANAGEMENT

"I am a little bit more famous now, but I have small change in my life. I live in the same place. I have the same friends."

Rafael Nadal

Consistent habits must be part of your life for longer than you think. If you are to succeed good habits must become part of the way you think. The more consistently you practice something the more professional you become. The most important habit is making sure you have switched on mentally before you practice. Warming up is not only for your body but also for your mind.

I try to instil consistent routines in players, not only so they become consistent on the court, but also so they become consistent off the court. Do not be frightened, because this doesn't take hours nor is it very difficult to do. It requires the desire to apply oneself for 5-10 minutes every day to be mentally ready to train. Let me repeat – every day. View this habit with the attitude of a reformed alcoholic, whose motto is:

"Each day is a recommitment to stay sober. Each day I have to prepare myself to be strong and resist the temptation of giving in to weakness and the short lived pleasure of a drink."

An alcoholic is trying to salvage his life and consistency is the key. As an athlete you lose little when you do not prepare mentally compared to the alcoholic, but the stakes can be high. Contemplate the following if you are extremely talented.

- Perhaps there is not enough at stake.

- Perhaps losing out on a top class career and the rewards that come with success are not enough. Perhaps the knowledge that you have let yourself down by not reaching your potential is not enough motivation.

- Perhaps consistent effort, giving of your best and the peace of mind that comes from that, is not enough to motivate you.

Okay, but then admit that you are perhaps a talented 'cruiser' – a good athlete rather than a dedicated athlete. This is not a crime and sadly it is often frowned upon when a player settles at a certain level. Yet in everyday life it is often applauded if a businessman decides he will not sacrifice more family time or leisure time to get further ahead. We call that getting out of the 'rat race' or 'work/life balance'. Becoming a professional athlete is the equivalent of operating in a 'rat race' environment that is possibly even tougher, with little sympathy for the constant intensity of focus. No wonder some athletes find a level of comfort and settle for this, which is a choice. This is in direct contradiction to earlier statements about not becoming complacent. To clarify, the difference between when it's okay to settle and when it isn't, is purely personal choice but honesty with yourself and your team is important so that goals and expectations are realistic to the efforts.

The habit of preparing mentally for each training session and getting focused on what you want to achieve is essential to not wasting time and gaining the small improvements that contribute to confidence and Locker Room Power.

Taking five to ten minutes day by day to ready yourself and focus on what you want is a healthy psyche that teaches the brain to cope on an ongoing basis.

Looking for the magic bullet, the one breakthrough that will make the difference, is the equivalent of dreaming about the fairy godmother coming at night and miraculously fixing everything. There are many people who believe that one day 'it will just happen', that somehow without consistent focus, discipline and work, success will follow automatically, without the pain of understanding their own mind.

The idea that progress happens without planning and execution on a regular basis is ludicrous. People do get better just because they are involved, but nowhere near the amount necessary to become an expert at anything. We need to be sure that, whatever we are doing, it is what we actually want to do, because we all do much better when we are having fun. Certainly not every part of training and work is fun, but if the core ingredient is passion then the tough stuff is palatable because we know that it will help our performance.

Quick points

- Talented players often fail to realise how much they are throwing away by not dedicating themselves to achieving good professional habits.
- Building consistent habits creates the comforting rituals that help players get mentally prepared for training sessions and matches.
- Developing routines for both before and after matches and practice gives athletes a sense of control.
- There is no fairy godmother who will "just make it happen".
- It is the small day-to-day gains that count.

- CHAPTER 26 -
IN AND OUT OF 'THE ZONE'

"It's tough, you have to push yourself ... it's not always an easy ride and you go through a few setbacks here and there. But then on a Saturday afternoon when you're lifting the trophy, everyone is still in their pyjamas watching you on television and you realise that those mornings are pretty worth it."

Maria Sharapova

The key to sustained success is the discipline to control excess emotion by remaining in the present and focusing as much as possible on the job at hand. This is often easier said than done!

Timothy Galway's The Inner Game explains that in essence we perform at our best when we are in the zone – tapped into our sub-conscious, basically performing out of our minds without conscious thought. We have all experienced this, and this book and many others offer some wonderful tools to help us attain this instinctive state. The aim is to be able to perform in this state regularly and under pressure. Although great champions can achieve this, even they struggle to be in the zone consistently. Top performers drop in and out of the zone but cleverly use time between points, changeovers or 'timeouts' to breathe, meditate, relax, and attempt to think clearly and regain some perspective. They are always looking for positive ways to work their way back into a match and back into the zone.

So how do we address the problem of how to perform under pressure when we have fallen out of the zone state, when our mind has become active and we are consciously aware of the inner conversation? No contest will be put on hold for us so we can re-establish the zone. In fact, opponents will sense the loss of focus and pile on the pressure if they are able.

When we fall out of this instinctive state we still need to bring something to the table to help us perform. I believe that the reason we lose this focus is because the ego becomes involved and allows negative influences or voices to invade our thoughts. At this point we need to bring positive ego traits to the battle to drown out the negative thoughts, rather than simply hoping to return to the zone. Positive ego traits include:

- Aggression
- Anger (short burst) to kick-start energy
- Positive statements
  (fist pump, positive noise on big shots and strong positive talk)
- Energised body language
- Conscious delivery of main weapons
- No reaction at all, but legs are energised and play is aggressive.

The environment that you practice in is very influential in creating self-control and resilience. Daily disciplines calm the mind to the point where it becomes abnormal to feel sorry for yourself, to have moods, or to express frequent emotion. Engineer constant thoughts and reminders that winning is normal, that raising standards is normal, and remember that win or lose, no one match, however important, is big enough to deter you from your chosen process. Learn and move on. This attitude if consistently applied is very helpful when players find themselves in stressful situations. The ability to cope with adversity in a calm way without feeling sorry for ourselves is a habit built in practice.

Quick points

- **Remain in the present and focus as much as possible on the job at hand.**
- **Learn to function effectively when you have fallen out of the zone.**
- **Use positive ego traits to keep your level of play high when the mind is trying to over-think.**
- **The training environment should encourage the ideas that winning, raising standards, learning and moving on from setbacks are normal reactions.**

- CHAPTER 27 -
EGO AND HUMILITY

"Discipline and diligence are up there on the list, but one of the most important qualities of many really successful people is humility. If you have a degree of humility about you, you have the ability to take advice, to be coachable, teachable. A humble person never stops learning."

Todd Blackledge - Vidal Sassoon

It may well be necessary to build up your ego first in order to muster the drive and ambition needed to succeed. However, once you have success it becomes obvious to many players that your ego can prevent you from attaining peace of mind with the success. Brash players such as Agassi in his early career, evolved and became aware of the privilege of success. Arrogance is replaced with assured confidence and humility. Role models such as Agassi understand the positive influence they can have on society and are appreciative of the people who have worked with them to achieve success.

Humility is actually more powerful than the ego. In reality very few people get close to being ego-less, but being aware of it as a goal will help you achieve greater balance and personal security.

One of the most significant factors about top performers is the capacity to find a way to perform when they are not in the zone. One of the ways they do this is by fully accepting that it is impossible to be in the zone at all times, particularly in high pressure performance situations. These zone experiences cannot possibly last as long as men's tennis matches at Grand Slam level, which are often over four hours long. A player may have a number of periods both in and out of the zone during a long match. Because of this, the most important thing top performers have learned is to completely accept that the real task is to still deliver a high quality competitive performance when they are uncomfortable, not in the zone and not playing well. This requires deep awareness and knowledge about the performance process at a high level, and the humility (or lack of ego) to accept and live this knowledge out on the court. Whilst the player must ultimately take responsibility for getting in to this state of mind, the coach's role in teaching this is vital. The coach must provide the right environment to allow this deep learning to occur. Learning to hang on positively when all seems lost takes years, not months. In fact, it is no exaggeration to say that it is a never-ending challenge, even for the best performers throughout the world of sport to understand and accept that they have to learn how to manage their mind when out of the zone.

A recent example of this was the final between Rafael Nadal and Juan Martin del Potro in Indian Wells in 2013. Nadal, at the start of the second set was not playing his best tennis and he was in danger of being overwhelmed by del Potro. However, he understood how important it was to dig in deep and allow himself time to get back into the match. For all that Nadal had achieved in tennis, he accepted that at that point during the match del Potro was the better player and he was humble enough to accept this. Nadal still managed to deliver some quality during the crisis at the start of the 2nd set to give him a fighting chance. He gradually improved his performance to get the victory, even though any observer of that match would categorically have said that through large parts of that match del Potro was the better player.

Quick points

- **Humility is more powerful than the ego.**
- **Top performers find ways to win even if it 'isn't their day'. They confront their egos and dig in.**
- **Learning to stay positive when all seems lost takes years, not months.**

- CHAPTER 28 -
SEPARATE SELF-BELIEF FROM CONFIDENCE

"I've always believed no matter how many shots I miss, I'm going to make the next one."

Isiah Thomas

Not one person achieves every goal they set, but one thing is guaranteed: an individual who has belief in their own abilities will always succeed to a higher level than someone who does not.

The basic belief that you will succeed is essential. This self-belief grows as you progress through different levels and achieve success. No person can believe in himself without achieving any victories. In order to have faith in yourself it is imperative that achievable goals are set. Consistently competing out of one's depth is a belief killer.

True self-belief develops over time when it becomes obvious why you are winning. It is born of a great intent to defeat opponents with your weapons and with the knowledge that you can consistently rely on these weapons. When this occurs, your opponents begin to fear the commitment behind the weapons you use and think about their own weaknesses.

When champions say they cannot believe they have won Wimbledon or Olympic gold, what they are actually saying is that they cannot believe how soon it happened or that what they had always believed in had finally happened! The fundamental belief that they could attain this goal was settled many years beforehand. When they consistently made enough quality balls they won matches, so breakthroughs are not a surprise.

Andy Murray is an example of a player who has always believed in himself. He has never had a problem visualizing himself competing at the very top level, so it is really no surprise to him when he gets there. He has always believed in himself as a person and a tennis player – this has been a key reason for his consistent success over the years, through the junior ranks and now on the Tour. His success confirms his self-belief and further strengthens it, so he becomes even more successful. Self-belief and success enhance each other – if you believe in yourself you are more likely to succeed; if you succeed you are more able to justify your self-belief and so on.

However, even champions have to go through a process of refining their skills and gaining the maturity to express their self-belief in a way that is powerful enough to win at the highest level.

Here is an example of Tim Henman realizing his coming of age as a player.

""When I beat the French Open champion, Yevgeny Kafelnikov, at Wimbledon (1996) in my first match on Centre Court, on the court that I'd always dreamed of playing on, saving two match points and going on to win in five sets, it changed my life forever. It is safe to say that when I walked back into the locker room after that match the other players looked at me differently and the respect was there. It is the day my Locker Room Power was established amongst the elite."

If you are aware that self-belief is just a decision to play point-by-point as hard as you can from the beginning to the end of the contest with enthusiasm (positive energy), whether you win or lose, then you will have an advantage because you will remain focussed on the task at hand throughout the course of a match. Many successful players, however, are purely instinctive. This means they can be rocked by events that occur throughout a contest, which can cause them temporarily to have doubts. Tiger Woods seemed to be an exception to this rule. He is a champion who has always appeared to have total belief no matter what surprises tested his faith and concentration. His private life rather than golfing challenges have affected his confidence, but my instinct says his basic belief is intact so he will go on to win again.

"My greatest point is my persistence. I never give up in a match. However down I am I fight until the last ball. My list of matches shows that I have turned a great many so-called irretrievable defeats into victories." - Björn Borg

The difference between the high achievers and the also-rans is not their work ethic or talents, but their self-belief. Most of us have two jobs in our quest for success: the job of learning how to believe and the job of getting better at what we do. The champion has only one job – the job of getting better. He has learnt to believe in himself regardless of whether he wins or

Separate Self-belief from Confidence

loses, while most of us fall into the trap of trying to be good enough before we can believe in ourselves.

The secret is that if you believe in yourself and lose, your only job is to keep getting better and when you are good enough, lack of self-belief is not going to prevent you from winning!

The myth is that if you believe in yourself and try hard enough, ultimately it will be enough to win. However, you cannot control whether or not you win, but you can control giving yourself the best opportunity to achieve a successful result. The key is to play from the beginning to the end of the match with 100% belief in making every ball. Only when the last point is won or lost is the contest over.

If you lose, you can then analyse what needs to be done better so that the next time you play that person you will be tougher, and when you are good enough you will win. Lewis Hamilton sums it up perfectly after losing the lead in the 2010 world drivers' championships at Monza after crashing out in an ill-fated attempt to pass Felipe Massa. Hamilton commented in his press conference following the event that "In bad situations you soak up all the lessons that need learning. You absorb that information, put the bad experiences to one side, use the benefits and move on." (BBC website Thursday, 16 September 2010)

By focusing on the task at hand instead of the result, you eliminate feelings of fear (e.g. 'I've got to win this game or else'). It has been said numerous times, but it is the process that matters, not the results. If the process is right, then the results will follow.

Being a strong person is looking at the cards you have been dealt and deciding to add up all the positive cards you hold. This is often just an adjustment of how you interpret the strengths and weaknesses of these cards. For instance, the story of the twin brothers, whose alcoholic father had been imprisoned for murder, exemplifies this point. Each brother had had the same upbringing and had had to face the same circumstances of a father in prison. One brother saw the circumstances of his father as a warning and became a successful lawyer; the other, unfortunately saw his father's actions as an example of a life he was destined to follow and ended up in prison for grievous bodily harm. When asked why they turned out the way they did, both brothers gave the same answer: 'With a father like mine what do you expect?' Each brother dealt with the same circumstances in very different ways.

Generally you hold a greater number of strong cards than you think, and often more than your opponent. A classic error is to assume your opponent is better prepared, mentally tougher, or simply better than you with little evidence other than your perception and imagination. A typical example of this is when you first catch a glimpse of your opponent and he or she looks threateningly tall or fit. Your mind instantly sends out warning signals, which you quickly need to replace with positive thoughts about your own game. If you believe in yourself you will be confident about playing your own game (using your cards) and seeing how the match unfolds before you make a judgment.

You may well be surprised how powerful you are and how weak the previously unchallenged opponent actually is. No matter what your background, you must be determined to put a positive spin on it – the choice is stark in its simplicity. Whatever your circumstances, you cannot afford to allow yourself to be a victim if your ambition is to be a champion. While there are places on earth and circumstances that severely limit opportunity, usually in the Western world opportunity abounds.

Below are some examples of situations that will test an athletes' self-belief.

Graph 1: Working hard to improve your game (foundation), but results are poor.

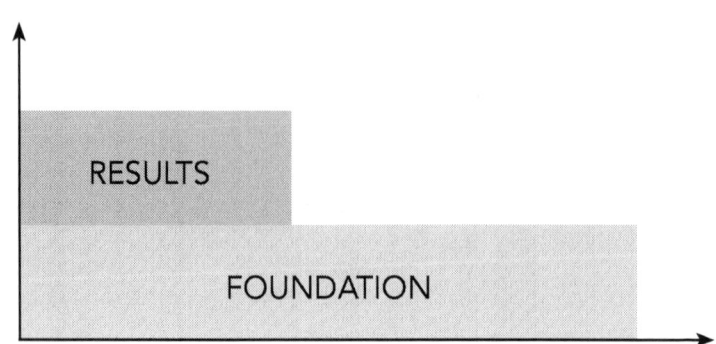

Graph 2: Player gets on a roll and confidence is so high that player overshoots their foundation - results are achieved at a level higher than expected.

Graph 3: If a player gets complacent or begins to have unrealistic expectations then after the first couple of losses there is a drain in confidence. The player will quickly bypass the foundation in a negative direction.

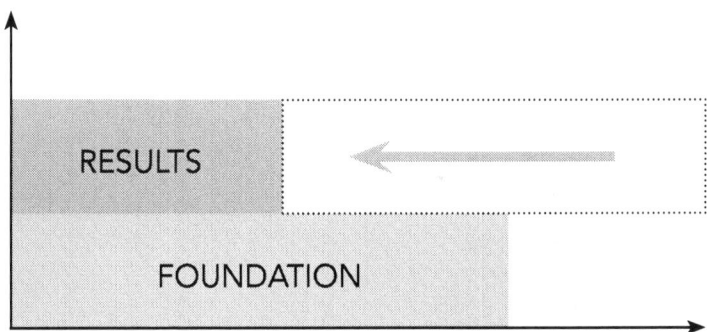

Confidence is low. Players will often bluff, blame and make excuses for this bad spell.

Expectation is high. The player tends to be sulky and ask questions like 'How can I lose to this guy'?

Anxiety is high. High stress detracts from good practice, further damaging game recovery.

Graph 4: The key is the attitude to the work and the understanding. Players and coaches need a spirit of continued respect for the process of learning.

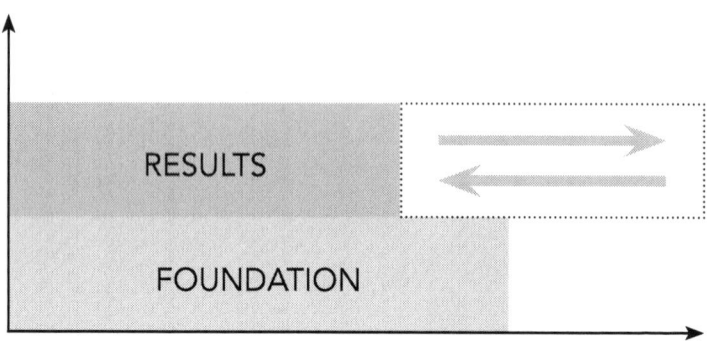

It is important to realise that equality between the foundation and results is never found. The ideal is steady improvement of the foundation and the results tend to fluctuate a few notches either way depending on confidence levels.

Basic Confidence is high and the dips are less dramatic. If the work ethic remains constant the process remains important, not only results.

Expectation is relative to the situation. The player and those around him have a good grip on where a player is and what can be achieved if things go right on the day.

Anxiety is generally under control. High stress detracts from good practice and although no player is ever without stress, the belief in their programme keeps a more laid-back attitude to challenges most of the time.

Quick points

- **Believe in yourself as a person as well as a player.**
- **Decide what you want to achieve.**
- **Focus on the task at hand, not the result.**
- **Question your game and your tactics but never your self-belief.**
- **Think positively – consider your glass to be half-full, not half-empty.**

- CHAPTER 29 -
DESIRE

*"What is the single most important quality in a tennis champion?
I would have to say desire, staying in there and winning matches
when you are not playing that well."*

John McEnroe

Desire gives you the motivation to do all the hard work involved in reaching your goal. It inspires you to do whatever is needed for however long it takes. Desire can be witnessed when the work rate and positive attitude does not drop off, regardless of winning or losing. Great desire is generally born out of great passion for your chosen vocation. It is difficult to be a champion in a profession that you hate, even if the profession is only a means to an end, such as material rewards. It is certainly less fulfilling when you have no passion for your work. However, there are examples of people who succeed in a profession that is not their passion, which is why desire and not passion is the first ingredient in the formula for success.

Desire grows with success and the growing realisation of what is possible. For example, it was certainly easier for Björn Borg to train six hours a day when he knew it would lead to more success. Compare his motivation to that of a perennial Wimbledon qualifier who knew that the end result for him was at best the possibility of a Wimbledon appearance, but most likely a loss in the qualifying tournament. Borg would practice in the knowledge that if he put in the sacrifice, he was giving himself the best chance to win another Wimbledon, which is no small motivation. For many players, reaching the main draw is tantamount to winning the lottery. After many years of unsuccessful attempts it is a rare individual who can approach their sport without some loss of expectation or desire, which is a sign that perhaps it's time to focus on a new direction.

In a frank and open discussion with Tim Henman about his experiences of Locker Room Power and his desire, he had this to say:

Question: *"Tim, did your desire grow over time?"*

Tim: *"The answer is definitely no. I knew from an early age that I wanted to be a professional player and this desire was strong throughout my career. My experience is that the exceptional achievers have a burning desire and love for their profession which seldom waivers. However there are athletes who slowly discover their talent and as they train and progress they gain confidence in their true prospects which ignites a desire to achieve. I knew from an early age that tennis was my love and even when, at 16, my coach sat me down and told me it would be best if I concentrated on my studies rather than try become a pro because he did not think I was good enough, I remember writing in my training diary that I had had a tough day at practice with my coach and that maybe I should modify my ambition to win Wimbledon to just becoming a pro tennis player. I was too embarrassed to write that my coach doubted my abilities, but even that did not deter me from following what I knew was my destiny, to be a pro. I realise now that this desire and knowing is exceptional at 17, especially given that my junior track record was anything but stellar, with little indication of the career that would follow."*

In his only appearance at junior Wimbledon in 1992, Tim lost 6-1, 6-2 in the first round. Most top players show their pedigree in the junior Grand Slams and in fact it is extremely rare for a player to make the top 100 having not been a world top 30 junior. Tim is one of a handful of these players and the most successful. My first recollection of the skinny lad from Oxfordshire was in 1992 during the U18 National Championships played in Nottingham. I was coaching Nick Baglin, a good athlete from Cheshire, who had risen from anonymity over the winter months when he had stunned Miles Maclagan to win a prestigious tournament. In the National Championships for U18s Nick beat a young Jamie Delgado in the quarterfinals and proceeded to make the final where he met another outsider, Tim Henman. Both players were not recognized as prime potential, nor did the final look to most coaches like anything other than an anomaly. It was Tim's balance, co-ordination; ability to volley and desire to volley that struck me. Tim won the match in four sets and although I was impressed, I certainly did not foresee a future top ten player. He had physical work to do and his game seemed lightweight. I felt Baglin had been mugged but in retrospect Tim actually handled the tournament calmly and with less fear than his contemporaries, a sign of the mental capacities he already possessed and would build to the point where he could mix it with the best in the world. It was his desire and belief that he would become a pro that was beginning to emerge in an understated way. Two years later he was taken seriously as a potential star.

I also encountered his steely focus during Davis Cup matches. Having coached Andy Richardson, Miles Maclagan, Jamie Delgado, Arvind Parmar and Barry Cowan to Davis Cup selection, I was privileged to be part of many teams and witnessed Tim getting ready to play. I distinctly remember standing next to him in the tunnel at Birmingham arena (2nd April 1999) before a match with Jim Courier, minutes before he was due on court. Music was blaring, the atmosphere was loud and electric, yet his eyes had changed and his game face was so much more mature and seasoned. The joking, relaxed and sociable guy who was immensely popular in the locker rooms of the world was gone and in his place was a professional killer. The change was palpable and he was only vaguely aware of the surrounding noise, his focus purely on the job ahead.

Quick points

- Desire is the single biggest motivator.
- For some people desire is in place at an early age, but for many, success and maturity begins to open opportunities that fuel a growing sense of purpose and desire.
- Desire keeps players going, keeps them strong when others doubt.
- A sense of destiny is evident in people who persevere against great odds to achieve their goals. The desire to achieve enables them to endure whatever it takes to break through.

- CHAPTER 30 -
PERSEVERANCE

"I have missed more than 9,000 shots in my career. I have lost almost 300 games. On 26 occasions I have been entrusted to take the game winning shot... and I missed. I have failed over and over and over again in my life. And that's precisely why I succeed."

Michael Jordan

Within the game of tennis, the perseverance it takes to become a champion is exceptional. To have the mental strength to go out and play regardless of what is happening in your personal life, if you're ill, not playing well or if you just don't feel like it, is immense. Very few have it; very few will ever have it.

"That's when you've got to grit your teeth and hang in there and try and find a way to win when you're not playing your best tennis - that's what I can be proud of."

Lleyton Hewitt

If we examine tennis champions and their pathway to the top of the game we begin to pick up clues as to how long and disciplined the journey can be. Becoming a champion takes time and experience. It takes years of repetition and learning, years of gaining personal power through knowledge, often gained from the disappointment of losing. Each time we learn and improve and control our thoughts under pressure, we begin to build the mind of a Champion. Star performers have a desire for success that becomes instinctive.

Champions come to terms with their abilities and mature from precocious to sublime talents. Pete Sampras won the US Open at 18 and then had two relatively poor years as he learned to harness his game and his status in the game before emerging as a wiser player who could use his talent rather than be at the mercy of it.

Roger Federer was slower to mature and at 22 won his first Slam at Wimbledon. Having already been through the process without winning a

Slam he was truly ready and was only missing the confidence that a player gains from winning a Slam. With this under his belt he immediately became prolific.

Andre Agassi had two careers. One as a precocious teen and young man who had little appreciation of the level of discipline required to be a prolific champion, which prevented him from owning the top spot, and one that began after a time of reflection. His talent was no different the second time round but his mental approach was, and thus his competitive spirit was unleashed on the tennis world in a far more organized and professional manner. This new manner was incredibly tough and consistent and allowed him to take his rightful place as a number one and an all-time great.

Quick points

- **Perseverance is not about changing your game overnight after a run of losses; you must learn, work and build to strengthen it.**
- **The journey from precocious talent to a Champion is long and arduous. It is not for the faint hearted because it is littered with disappointment.**

- CHAPTER 31 -
SUCCESS

"You have to find it. No one else can find it for you."

Björn Borg

Success is personal. You define it. You choose its measure. Whatever your circumstances, the choice remains the same – you can choose to be a victim or a survivor. If you view yourself as doing well according to your criteria then you are successful, because your achievement is totally relevant to your own context. For example, if a holy man passes through a whole day without a negative thought about any person, he may view that as the most successful day of his life. Similarly, someone who chooses to work the land and be self-sufficient in life will view his existence as thriving on the day he achieves self-sufficiency. For some, waking up each morning is success – all they need is the gift of life to feel great.

The limits of success are not set in stone. Upon achieving a goal you may wish to set a new target to measure against. If you want to guarantee an uneasy, unsuccessful life, then measure your success against other people who are always ahead of you. A much better way of experiencing realisation is to know what it means to you. Set your own personally-oriented goals and then focus on accomplishing them. Be wary, however, not to use a low measure of success as a cop-out. Achieving soft accomplishments is not rewarding. If Roger Federer played challenger tournaments his entire career, he would be avoiding the ultimate challenges to his talents that the Tour provides. The best feeling in the world is when we make progress and win, overcoming the pain and hurt of prior disappointments This is a high that makes the hard journey worth every second. This is true of any achievement we have worked towards, no matter where, when or what. The joy of overcoming challenges is the nectar of life.

Go wholeheartedly after your desire and compete with the right attitude. Believe in yourself and approach the task with the maturity to accept the defeats that will come your way as part of the journey. You must also realise that it is not guaranteed that every ambition will be accomplished. As mentioned previously, life is not an even playing field and it starts genetically with the physical gifts you are given, which preclude many people from being professional sport stars. However, this does not mean that great personal satisfaction cannot be gained from taking part in sport and excelling at different levels. For example, the achievement of the Paralympic 100 metre sprinter is no less rewarding to him, even though it is slower than his able-bodied counterpart.

In order to compete with self-belief you need to put success into your own context and be true to yourself. For instance, if you are a subsistence farmer but deep down your aim was to be a large commercial farmer, you will never fulfill your dreams. You may pretend to be happy with your lot in life without ever going after the goal of becoming a commercial farmer, but this is a recipe for cynicism, which is far worse than living with the disappointment of not achieving as much as you might have liked. At least if you are true to yourself, you will travel along the right path and reap the rewards of believing in your actions.

Being defeated or never achieving an ultimate goal is not failure. Striving for success is a victory in itself. You can never guarantee winning as there are so many variables in sport. Also, there can only be one number one or winner of a tournament.

"I have always said that I want to finish my career with the Dolphins and this put me closer to that goal. I have been fortunate to break many personal records, but my overriding goal is to win a Super Bowl here in Miami."

Dan Marino

Dan Marino, the great quarterback, is a fine example of someone who achieved success without ever achieving his goal. He chose to spend his career attempting to win the Super Bowl with the Miami Dolphins, never to achieve this ambition. However, his loyalty to Miami was rewarded with a life-long respect and love from the Miami football community. The success achieved on his journey may in the end prove more valuable to Dan than any Super Bowl success. Had he won the Super Bowl, this would undoubtedly have been the icing on the cake, but no one will deny that he has been successful in his quest.

By committing himself wholeheartedly to his ambition Dan Marino achieved success.

"If you ask any great player or great quarterback, there's a certain inner confidence that you're as good as anybody. But you can't say who the absolute best is. To be considered is special in itself."

The twists and turns of the journey can take you to places you never imagined and give you opportunities to meet people who become very important to you, even if your goal is not achieved. Your journey may even lead you into changing your goal and enable you to achieve a different type of success that gives greater personal satisfaction than you could ever imagine.

Quick points

- **Remember that success is committing yourself fully to your goal. The result is a bonus.**
- **Success is Personal. You define it. You measure it.**
- **Being defeated or never achieving an ultimate goal is not failure. Striving for success is a victory in itself.**
- **The twists and turns of the journey can take you to places you never imagined.**

- CHAPTER 32 -
SAMMELISM'S

In wrapping up the book I will outline a few Sammelism's, points that over time I know help athletes on their wonderful yet tough journey to become the best they can be. This book is a reference book, something you reread, make notes in and underline or highlight. It is not the only good book on improving your mind, but it is one of the few that give you not only the 'what', but 'the how' with practical tools to use daily.

- In a match, looking desperately to your coach for help is counterproductive. Even if she can and does help you, who then owns your toughness? Do not confuse the help of a coach as something that can save you. The aim is to own and believe in your own toughness.

- There is no fairy godmother. So many players believe that one day they will wake up in the morning 'mentally tough' having been visited by the fairy godmother during the night, who magically solved their problems. They fail to work hard on the process of becoming tough, living in the fantasy that one day it just happens. Each day that passes in hope is a day wasted.

- Sport owes you nothing. Expectations of what should or should not happen just because you think you have worked harder/tried harder/done anything harder than others is rubbish.

- Genuinely work hard and good things will happen, you just can't predict when.

- True Locker Room Power is gained when you enjoy the competition and fight with an optimistic attitude no matter what the score. Respect steadily grows the longer you sustain this mentality.

- Commitment pressure is cumulative. Play your game with intent from the start. Use your weapons and make statements early. Rewards come later in a match due to consistent commitment to your game. This is especially true when losing - keep committed to the end, as you never know when the cracks will appear due to cumulative pressure.

- Never switch off in a point. Disaster happens when a point is all but won and a player switches off and carelessly misses an easy finish because in his mind the point is over. It is not over until it is totally finished.

- Work hard, but let things come to you. This is the hardest concept to master. Whether it is a point or a career, you cannot force things to happen. You work hard and allow points or a career to open up for you. Proactively go after things, do everything in your power to succeed and allow things to happen… trying to force things will increase the resistance. Trying to force a door down is tiring and stressful. Keep knocking with greater offerings ie, keep improving until what you have to sell is irresistible and the door will open.

- People do change all the time. I hate the belief that people don't change. Has not every person evolved? Have champions not adapted and grown in strength both in the mind and in the game? Fat people can lose weight. Weak people can become strong in adversity. Poor can become rich. Selfish people can become philanthropists. Unfit people can become marathon runners. The proof of change is all around us. Whatever you want to improve, you can!

- Everything is perception of actions. Wimbledon is a great tournament because of its history, prestige and universal agreement. Take away the prize-money, stop improving facilities, and in time it would become "once was a great tournament". Perceptions change – so how you are perceived can be changed by different actions.

- Happiness is gratitude. If you are grateful for who you are and what you have then you are happy. Gratitude for your life is your perception of it. It is a choice.

- Mental toughness is a decision.

- Trust yourself and your game will evolve with hard work. A top junior who trusts his game will have insecurities at pro level until he improves enough to compete with the pros. Trust in yourself is gained by knowing you will do what needs to be done.

- Feeling sorry for yourself is a waste of time. Competing with excellence is no place for self-pity. Moving on after each disappointment is the key to getting stronger. Learn and move on without the negative residue that further drains confidence. Repair from a loss is best attained through a good practice session.

- CHAPTER 33 -
THEORETICAL UNDERPINNING BY LOUISE SCOTT, MSc BSc

What Dave Sammel discusses throughout this book is applied sport psychology. Applied sport psychology is underpinned by various psychological theories. These theories have been adapted to make them relevant to the sporting world. Although Dave is not a qualified sport psychologist, because of his involvement as an elite coach within the world of professional sport, Dave's experience and knowledge is thorough and great. Indeed there are many coaches around the world who deliver psychological support to their athletes. And, it is the opinion of some sport psychologists (e.g. Nesti, 2004) who firmly believe that coaches are in the best position to deliver sport psychology techniques known as mental skills. Mental skills such as imagery, self-talk, relaxation techniques and goal setting come under the realm of psychological skills training. As researchers, consultants and coaches become more experienced they tend to favour a particular approach or theory, whilst others, such as Dave, have an eclectic approach. As such they take aspects from various psychological theories (e.g. existentialism, cognitive behavioural, humanistic and coaching development) and weave them together to form a theory that best suits them. For instance, cognitive psychology underpins what Dave does with goal setting, whereas chapters such as being In or Out of the Zone are underpinned by existential psychology. In fact it is this approach (existential psychology) that underpins the majority of Dave's work.

Existential psychology is based on a theory that psychology is a human science (Giorgi, 1970). As a result this theory focusses on the person first and the athlete second. Its mantra is that by creating an excellent person, you will create an excellent athlete. One of the main characteristics of existential psychology is that it demands the individual to take a holistic approach. Therefore it does not isolate the human being; it studies them in various environments and cultures. Dave is not only concerned about his players when they're on the court, he is interested in their whole persona, both on and off the court. Dave trains and works with people who play tennis, not just tennis players. Existential psychology acknowledges that both positive and negative events and experiences can benefit the development of persons in sport and life as a whole (Nesti, 2010). This fits the realms of tennis well, as players can experience such extraordinary highs one week and in the next capitulate. Perhaps the most important facet of this brand of psychology is the acceptance that anxiety can be a positive experience. Existential theorists do not restrict themselves to purely competitive anxiety, quite the contrary in-fact. These theorists look at and inspect the anxieties of life. They understand and accept that the anxieties life can absolutely impact on the performance of athletes. However rather than try to disperse this emotion from our world the existential approach suggests that anxiety should be faced and used beneficially to aid decision-making and to help the individual accept responsibility. In fact, this belief that anxiety is predominately a negative emotion is being challenged by cognitive behavioural psychologists. Numerous researchers (e.g. Hardy and Parfitt, 1991; Hardy, 1997; Woodman, Albinson, and Hardy, 1997) argued against the 'myth' that anxiety is always detrimental to performance. Indeed the studies listed above indicated in their results that some of the athletes who participated were shown to perform better when they were cognitively anxious, leading to latest conceptualization that anxiety can be either debilitative or facilitative on performance depending on the individual athlete. Within the world of competitive sports we have all heard those stories from elite athletes who have been physically sick with nerves and anxiety before they compete, but they understand that it is the right place in order for them to perform at their maximum. This development with regards to anxiety has brought the cognitive behavioural approach and the existential approach closer together. The existential also has two different types of anxiety: normal and neurotic. Existential psychologists (e.g. May, 1977) believe that normal anxiety, which comes as a result of life's trials and tribulations, is healthy and attributed to personal growth. Neurotic anxiety is debilitative and occurs when a person fails to meet the challenge of normal anxiety. The main difference between the two approaches is that the cognitive approach would attempt to relieve athletes of this anxiety by using various mental skill techniques, whereas the existential approach helps people face this anxiety and aids them in accepting it as part of everyday life. In order to face the anxiety of life, existential psychologists encourage their clients to engage in self-examination. This self-examination will result in the individual having greater levels of self-knowledge and self-awareness (Nesti, 2004).

The rest of this chapter will look at the theoretical underpinning of a number of other chapters in this book, notably: In and Out of The Zone, Courage and Self-Belief.

In and Out of The Zone

'He's in the zone'. A statement made many times by observers of elite sport. Some readers of this book may have experienced being in the zone. They may also say that during this period of time it was the best they have ever performed. They may not have been victorious but their performance was something to be remembered. Within the sport psychology literature, this psychological state, commonly known as the zone, is defined as 'flow' (Csikszentmihalyi, 1975, 1982, 1990, 1997). Flow is grounded within humanistic psychology and philosophy. Flow is an optimal psychological state that occurs when there is a balance between perceived challenges and skills in an activity (Csikszentmihalyi, 1990). It is a state of concentration so focused that it amounts to a complete absorption in an activity an individual is undertaking. Ultimately flow is viewed as a peak performance state, and various researchers have supported this (e.g. Jackson and Roberts, 1992).

Enjoyment and intrinsic motivation are essential requirements for Csikszentmihalyi's (1975) theory of flow. Many activities have the ability to stimulate the flow experience, however an individual needs to feel intrinsically rewarded by their activity in order to achieve the flow experience. Researchers (e.g. Csikszentmihalyi, 1975, 1990, 1997; Jackson, 1992; Hefferon and Ollis, 2006) have supported the suggested nine characteristics of flow, which are:

- The activity must be enjoyable.
- The individual must perceive that they have the ability to meet the demands of the task (e.g. they can compete and win).
- Total absorption in the task, individuals lose conscious thought over their actions.
- Loss of self-consciousness.
- Movements and actions become spontaneous.
- Full concentration on the task at hand.

- Individuals feel a heightened sense of control.
- Loss of the sense of time, minutes seem like seconds.
- You have a specific, achievable goal in your mind.

As the flow state is believed to lead to an athlete's optimal performance, existential psychologists work with athletes to help them reach and achieve flow states. However these psychologists will not use anxiety-excluding techniques, because they believe that anxiety is a normal part of sport and is attributed to personal growth. As a result we should embrace and accept it. The existential approach to psychology suggests that by improving an athlete's self-knowledge and self-awareness their performance will improve (Corlett, 1996a; Miller and Kerr, 2002). Athletes should engage in a process of self-examination, which, if done properly, will result in a greater knowledge of the self. Once the individual has greater awareness and knowledge of themselves they will be able to face the anxieties of everyday life and, what's more, they can utilise them in a positive manner.

In order for athletes to enter the 'zone' more frequently the process of self-examination is one they should engage in. Dave allows his players to walk down many avenues that provoke wholehearted self-examination.

Courage

Courage within the domain of sport psychology is a relatively new threshold. However the characteristic of courage has been around for thousands of years. For the ancient Greeks, courage was a part of virtuous living. Courage is one of the virtues that Greek philosophers valued, the others being wisdom, humanity, justice, temperance and transcendence (Park and Peterson, 2004). In ancient times courage was considered a vital component of a human being's make-up and character, as it took courage to live and survive in those days, whereas Corlett (2002) noted that in today's modern world courage is seen as a skill and instrument to benefit from. Over the years there have been various conceptualisations of courage, such as the one offered by Park and Peterson (2004). The authors classified courage as emotional strength that involves the exercise of will to accomplish goals in the face of opposition. This consists of bravery, perseverance, honesty and vitality.

Throughout Sam's interview regarding courage she mentioned that a courageous act is associated with a level of fear. This is acknowledged in Woodard and Pury (2007) definition of courage: "the voluntary willingness to act with or without varying levels of fear, in response to a threat to achieve an important, perhaps moral, outcome or goal".

Within the context of sport, athletes present many different forms of courage (Konter and Ng, 2012). Indeed, Konter and Ng (2012) indicated that athletes who break records and take great risks whilst challenging their opponents in the competitive arena are examples of courage in the sporting arena. Other examples of courage within sport are such things as returning to the same level of competition after serious injury, continuation after grieving for a loved-one, and promoting social change. Additionally the process of self-examination, which was mentioned in the previous section, may also be a form of courage, albeit a less obvious form. Nesti (2010) suggested that if a player takes the time to examine themselves, their performances, their mentality and how others perceive them it requires a large degree of courage, because the individual may not like what they find. This act is a courageous one as the athlete is looking for areas to improve in both their sporting life and their general life. Nesti (2010) has stated that for "a player to engage in looking closely at who they are takes great courage and self-discipline" (pg. 49-TBC). Ultimately the value of courage cannot be underestimated within sport and indeed life. Corlett (1996b) has highlighted its importance by noting that courage is something of a necessity to the continual development and achievement of high-level sport performers.

Self-Belief

"The whole thing is never to get negative about yourself. Sure, it's possible that the other guy you're playing is tough and that he may have beaten you the last time you played, and okay, maybe you haven't been playing all that well yourself. But the minute you start thinking about these things you're dead. I go out to win every match convinced that I'm going to win. That's all there is to it."

Jimmy Connors (cited in Weinberg, 1988, p.127)

Self-belief and self-confidence are perhaps the ultimate qualities for any athlete to have. These qualities can be tough to get and extremely easy to lose. These two qualities are often thrown around within the same concept. However they do differ somewhat. Self-belief falls under Bandura's Self Efficacy Theory (1977). Self-efficacy theory, the perception of one's ability to perform a task successfully, is really a micro-level approach or situation-specific form of confidence. It investigates the individual's perceived ability to perform a specific skill, e.g. hitting a drop-shot off the backhand side or kicking a top-spin serve out to the opponent's backhand. Contrastingly, overall confidence falls under the sport confidence macro level approach generated by Vealey (1986). This universal approach is associated with overall performance expectancies in sport e.g. can I win? In later years Bandura (1997) altered his definition of self-efficacy to include one's perceived abilities to overcome obstacles or challenges to perform successfully, e.g. running 10 miles in the winter. This new definition became known as self-regulatory efficacy. Efficacy perceptions are crucial to human processes because people's levels of motivation, affective states, and related actions are based on what they believe to be true rather than the reality of what is true (Bandura, 2000).

An athlete's feeling of self-efficacy is based on six principal sources of information:

- **Performance accomplishments (based on mastery experiences).**
- **Vicarious experiences.**
- **Verbal persuasion.**
- **Imagined experiences.**
- **Physiological states.**
- **Emotional states.**

Some of these sources of information are more influential on an individual's efficacy perception than others. For instance several researchers have established that mastery experiences have the greatest impact on self-efficacy perception in sport (Bandura, 1997; Myers, Feltz, and Short, 2004; Myers and Feltz, 2007). Morris and Koehn (2004) concluded that those individuals (regardless of whether they participated in a team or individual sport) who indicated that they had high self-efficacy levels were associated with superior performances.

BACKGROUND

David Sammel (BA Econ and English)

David Sammel is currently Head Coach of TeamBath Academy and ATP Tour coach with vast experience in coaching international players. He has coached over a dozen players to represent their countries in The Davis Cup, Federation Cup and two Olympians.

He has conducted Locker Room Power workshops for several Premier Football League clubs including Chelsea and Fulham and is a sought-after speaker and presenter. He also works psychologically with athletes from several sports on an individual basis.

Louise Scott (MSc; BSc Applied Sport Psychology)

Louise is currently Head of Sport Science and Futsal Coordinator/Girls Centre of Excellence Manager at Sporting Club Albion, part of West Bromwich Albion FC. She was Research Assistant to Dr Chris Harwood on the tennis parents' project at Loughborough University in 2013 and is a qualified tennis coach.

GLOSSARY

The pathway in tennis involves a number of organizations and governing bodies. Here is a brief glossary and explanation of this often complex world.

Each country has a governing body that oversees tennis.

- In the UK it is the Lawn Tennis Association (LTA) and in the USA it is the United States Tennis Association (USTA)

- The International Tennis Federation (ITF) governs the Olympics, Davis Cup (Men) and Federation Cup (Female) - both annual international team competitions to determine the world champion country.

- The Grand Slams are the Australian Open, French Open, Wimbledon and US Open. The Australian and US Open are played on hard courts, the French on clay, and Wimbledon is on grass. All are run separately, and are part of the Grand Slam committee, but played under the rules of the ITF.

The pathway through tennis is as follows:

- Junior and senior tournaments sanctioned by each country's governing body.

- Europe has a series of international junior tournaments at under 16, under 14 and under 12 age groups, sanctioned and run by Tennis Europe (TE).

- The ITF administer the World Juniors, which is an Under 18 circuit and produces the U18 world rankings.

- The ITF also administer the bottom rungs of professional tennis called Futures, currently men's $15,000 and $25,000 tournaments. The ITF also manage the women's $15,000 and Challenger tour, ranging from $25,000 to $100,000.

- The Association of Tennis Professionals (ATP) runs the men's Challenger tour and the main pro tour including the Master's series.

- The Women's Tennis Association (WTA) runs the women's pro tour.
- Both the ATP and WTA are solely responsible for the pro world rankings, which are issued weekly, except during the middle of the Grand Slams, Indian Wells and Miami Masters run over two weeks.

In a nutshell:

- Domestic tennis and tournaments are run by countries' governing bodies.
- U16, U14, U12 International in Europe – TE.
- U18 International tournaments – ITF.
- Futures (Pros.) – ITF.
- Challengers (Female Pros.) – ITF.
- Challengers (Male Pros.) – ATP.
- Pro Tour - ATP/WTA.
- Grand Slams/Davis Cup/Federation Cup/Olympics – ITF

Your Notes & Inspiration:

"David Sammel is an International Tennis Coach and a widely respected Consultant across the spectrum of professional sport. He is the creator of the coaching philosophy that is known as Locker Room Power."

Printed in Poland
by Amazon Fulfillment
Poland Sp. z o.o., Wrocław